sew4home™
Bags and Totes

10 Easy, Fashionable Projects Anyone Can Sew

sew4home™
Bags and Totes

10 Easy, Fashionable Projects Anyone Can Sew

Liz Johnson and Anne Adams
Founders & Managing Editors of Sew4Home

Fons&Porter
CINCINNATI, OHIO

Contents

Introduction

Want it? Make it! When we started *Sew4Home* in 2009, our goal was to encourage people who'd never even switched on a sewing machine to become avid sewers. We wanted to give our website visitors the confidence to produce projects that looked as good as, if not better than, the items they drooled over on the shelves of stores and in the pages of catalogs and magazines. To that end, we dedicated Sew4Home.com to providing the most detailed, step-by-step project instructions and accompanying techniques. The kind that make you shout, "I finally get it! I can do that!" And we do it without ever sacrificing style or flair. So your friends can shout, "Wow! You made that?"

Our projects struck a chord not only with those just starting out but also with seasoned sewing enthusiasts who love our creativity and are just as happy for the thorough instructions. With nearly a half million people from around the world visiting the site each day, it's thrilling to now reach out with our first book, inspiring a whole new group to make what they want with confidence and style.

We looked through our most popular projects online and decided this book should cover bags and totes. It's a fact—we all need something to carry our stuff, and although a simple paper bag might do the job, it doesn't exactly make our hearts go pitter-patter. Who doesn't love a great bag or tote? Even if we have several, there's always room for one (or two or three) more. Here's the good news about making your own: Bags have many underlying construction similarities.

Learn the basics, and your originals can compete with bags costing hundreds of dollars. And you can make it for a fraction of the price in *your* favorite materials.

So what creates that professional finish? It's a combination of having the proper tools and truly understanding the techniques that add the finishing details. We show you how to avoid common mistakes and give you the secrets to choosing fabric and hardware that bring it all together.

Part of the fun is being exposed to the variety and versatility of different fabric substrates. Don't restrict yourself to the quilting cotton aisle. Learn to work with linen, canvas, faux leather and more. Today's faux fabrics can be nearly impossible to distinguish from the real thing, but they're so much easier to work with—as well as much more humane.

Our hope is that by providing beautiful projects, you are inspired to create. And by making those projects accessible and understandable, you have the confidence to move from just thinking about making something to actually finishing a project, and then another, and another.... The ultimate goal is to have you share your love of sewing with someone else who has yet to experience the lure of needle and thread. Just as you can never have too many bags, you can never have too many creators. It makes the world a much more beautiful place.

—Anne and Liz

Helpful Tips, Handy Techniques & Cool Hardware

The products you choose to work with are important to both achieving a professional finish and implementing a smooth and efficient process along the way to that pro finish. Using great tools eliminates frustration and frees up your creativity. This section of the book gives you an overview of the basic elements you need to get started along with a few premium options to consider for the best possible results. We'll also touch on sewing techniques that streamline the construction process and share our thoughts on working with color, texture and design.

Measuring

One of the first things you do in any project is measure. Of course, the more accurate your measurements, the better your end results. The carpenter's words of wisdom, "Measure twice, cut once" are just as important for sewing.

Ruler: Get a see-through ruler that's at least 12" (30.5cm) long. A transparent ruler lets you see what you're measuring and gives you accurate horizontal and vertical lines. You'll also need the hard, straight edge for cutting with a rotary cutter.

Tape measure: The classic sewing notion. Get one that is flexible but not stretchy. You'll use it for measuring three-dimensional objects, working with long cuts of fabric, aligning patterns and more.

Seam gauge: This handy little fella is a small ruler (usually 6" [15cm] total) with a double-pointed, sliding guide. It's great for marking seam allowances and hems or using anytime you need to set and then repeatedly check a small measurement.

Premium options: Consider adding transparent rulers in specialty shapes, such as squares, frames and triangles. We also love hemming guides and gauges.

Marking

Being able to draw a straight line to follow or to indicate the exact spot for a snap means you need to mark on your fabric. Sounds scary, right? Only if you're considering using a permanent marker. There are special tools just for marking on fabric. Important tip: Always test your marking tool on a scrap of the actual project fabric(s) before using it on your project.

Pen: A water-soluble marking pen allows you to draw on your fabric, then wash out the ink or wipe it away with a damp cloth.

Pencil: Fabric pencils have special "lead" that also easily washes out. White pencils show up on dark fabric. Dark pencils are for light fabrics. Some pencils come with their own specialty erasers and brushes that make eliminating the lines even easier. A regular pencil sharpener will keep a nice point on your fabric pencils.

Premium options: Air-soluble pens (which dissolve/vanish over time with exposure to the air) and heat-soluble pens (you can iron off the ink) are good additions so you don't always have to wash/wet the item to remove your markings.

Cutting

Remember when your mom yelled at you for using her "good scissors?" Now you'll understand. Sharp, precise cutting tools are very important. Once you have your favorites, don't use them to cut anything but fabric! Even paper cutting will quickly dull good sewing scissors.

Scissors and shears: Get a good pair of shears for fabric cutting in a standard straight-blade option. If you'll be doing a lot of cutting and prefer scissors over a rotary cutter, you may want to add a pair of bent dressmaker shears. They have a bend of about 45° at the pivot point for a more ergonomic cutting position.

Seam ripper: This allows you to undo your sewing mistakes. A good seam ripper is invaluable and not very expensive. Don't necessarily rely on the one that came with your machine; make sure yours is super sharp.

Rotary cutter: These are nifty for curves, long slices and exact cuts against a straight edge (remember those see-through rulers above). They work similar to a pizza cutter, and many people prefer them to scissors. Two things to remember: Always use rotary cutters on a cutting mat or you could cut right through your fabric and into your work surface, and these blades are sharp when new; always cover and lock the blade when not in use.

Cutting mats: You must have one of these to use your rotary cutter. But you'll also find the lines and markings useful for general cutting and marking. A medium size, about 18" x 24" (45.5cm x 61cm), is good when starting out. Get the type that is labeled as "self-healing" to keep the surface smoother for a longer period of time.

Premium options: Tiny sharp snips are great for getting into small corners and curves. And the more you sew, you'll find there's almost no such thing as a cutting mat that is too big.

Measuring, marking, pressing and cutting tools. Clockwise from upper left: shears, rotary cutter, pressing cloth and ham, iron, snips, marking pens and pencils, clear rulers, tape measure, seam gauge, seam ripper and specialty template shapes.

Pressing

If you want your projects to look professional, you gotta apply a little pressure. Well-pressed seams are what give a project those wonderful crisp, clean edges. And don't we all love to erase wrinkles?

Steam iron: Get a good one. If you have an old one that doesn't heat up well or dribbles water, get a new one. Look for one that lets you control the amount of steam, from none to a big blast of heat and spray.

Ironing board: These come in all sizes; choose the one that will be best for your work space and is at your preferred height. Some folks like to stand at a traditional ironing board, others prefer a portable style and some people choose the smaller ironing pads. You want a surface that is firm and sturdy, padded well and cotton-covered.

Ham: Pressing hams are handy three-dimensional, fabric-stuffed shapes that help you iron curves and other hard-to-reach areas.

Pressing cloths: Some types of fabric have a tendency to shine (or even melt) if heat is applied directly; a pressing cloth can help prevent that. Choose a cloth made from natural fiber such as cotton or wool, or make your own.

Premium options: A mini iron is great to get into tight places a regular iron just can't go.

Needles, Pins and Thread

At its core, sewing is simply passing needle and thread through fabric. But this means the needles, pins and thread you choose are important. The variety is almost overwhelming, but start with quality basics and you'll never be disappointed.

Sewing-machine needles: The rule of thumb is to start every new project with a new needle. It's like sharpening your pencil before you write. Start with universal needles for most woven fabrics in an 80/12 size. A needle size has two numbers, such as 75/11 or 80/12. The first number is a European designation; the second is American. For a light-weight fabric, choose a small number (e.g., 70/10); for a heavy fabric, choose a large number (e.g., 90/14).

Hand-sewing needles: Get a variety pack of hand-sewing needles that gives you several point styles and eye sizes.

Needle threader: These are inexpensive and will save you a lot of frustration. They consist of a thin wire loop on a fob. Insert the loop through the needle's eye, thread this much larger and easier-to-see loop, then pull it back through the eye. You can use these for hand- or sewing-machine needles.

Thread: This is a *huge* category, and it seems a little crazy to try to condense it into one paragraph. In general, good quality thread from a major manufacturer will run better in your machine. Don't worry about having a huge collection to start with. For most projects, all-purpose thread in your top spool and bobbin is a safe bet.

Pins and pincushion: Get steel straight pins with the colored balls on the top. They're easier to insert, see and pick up when you spill them all over the floor. A magnetic pin dish is great to hold your entire collection. Then keep a stuffed pincushion next to your machine to hold a few pins while you're working. Some specialty fabrics are better secured with clips. We like the Clover Wonder Clips and Dritz Getta Grip clips for faux leather and vinyl.

Premium options: The main upgrade here is variety. As you expand your sewing skills, you'll want to add more sizes of needles and pins and more colors and types of thread, from silky rayon to soft cotton to sparkling metallic.

Needles, pins and thread. Clockwise from upper left: standard thread spools, straight pins, pincushion, hand-sewing needles and threader, specialty thread spools, sewing-machine needles and construction clips.

The Machine and Its Presser Feet

Your machine is your largest and most important tool. Just because a sewing machine runs doesn't mean you're going to want to spend time sewing on it. A garage-sale machine or something you've dug out from the back of Grandma's closet can add more to your frustration level than anything it might save on cost. Even the simplest seam requires dozens of parts in the machine to be moving at hundreds of revolutions per minute—all in perfect sync. Anything that's slightly off results in skipped stitches, thread tangles and big headaches.

You don't have to break the bank and buy the most expensive machine available, but you should buy the best machine you can possibly afford. First and foremost, you want a machine that makes good quality stitches. You also want something that's easy to use from the very beginning. You don't want to have to relearn the machine each time you start a new project. Some features we always look for include: automatic buttonholes, a superior fabric-feeding system that can accommodate thicker fabrics and an automatic needle threader.

Also look for a good complement of specialty presser feet. On our must-have list for bag construction are:

Zipper foot: Use this foot for inserting zippers as well as attaching trims.

Walking or even-feed foot: It adds fabric feeding power to the foot itself, giving you top and bottom control, which is awesome for handling thick layers.

Quarter-inch seam foot: This is a lifesaver for precise seams.

Nonstick foot: This is great for sewing with specialty substrates, such as faux leathers and laminates.

Clear-view foot: You can see through this foot, which is a big help when topstitching.

Fabric and Interfacings

The projects in this book feature a variety of fabric types, called "fabric substrates" in the trade. Premium quality, 100% cotton is the largest category in the fabric universe, but the alternative substrates are invaluable to bag construction where heavier materials are often important.

Canvas, faux leather, vinyl, linen and polyester all have their place. We provide supply details for each project, and our Resources section at the end of the book contains several where-to-buy options. The width of the fabric required for each project is 45" (114.5cm) unless otherwise noted in the materials list.

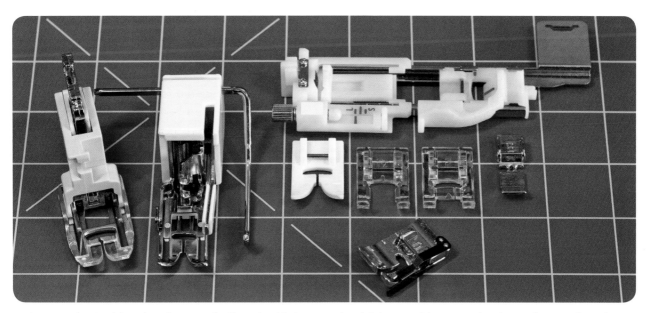

Machine presser feet. From left to right: walking or even-feed foot (with quilt bar), automatic buttonhole foot, nonstick foot, open-toe foot, clear-view foot, zipper foot and quarter-inch seam foot.

Each project also includes a list of the proper interfacing(s) that will give the specific bag or tote its shape and structure. Simply put, interfacing is a textile that goes behind your fabric (or between the fabric layers) to give it the support it needs to look good and hold up well. Interfacing comes in a huge variety of options: woven or nonwoven, thick or sheer, fusible or sew-in, packaged or on a bolt. The width of the interfacing required for each project is 45" (114.5cm) unless otherwise noted in the materials list.

Hardware and Closures

Not everything in sewing is soft. We want to talk just a bit about the hardware and closures that are the finishing touch on many bags and totes. Here's a little secret about these bad boys: Even though they include multiple parts—sometimes moving parts—and require a few extra tools to install, the actual process is easy. The key is confirming the placement of the pieces (usually two halves), but that's just a matter of careful measuring and double-checking. And sometimes, you get to hit things with a hammer, which is great for releasing tension.

Zippers: They're not as frightening as you think, and putting them in bags and totes is usually much easier than inserting them in garment construction.

D-rings, sliders and swivel hooks: These are the elements that make up most straps and handles. They are usually metal but are sometimes heavy plastic.

Magnetic snaps: These are the go-to closure for a majority of bags.

Twist and push locks: Next up on the closure food chain, twist locks and push locks make very pretty options for flaps and more. These come in a variety of types, including the flip, pivot and press locks shown below.

Grommets, eyelets and standard snaps: Since these are usually installed with large presses in commercial production, people think they can't replicate the look at home. Wrong! Not only can you do it, it's easy and rather fun. A well-placed metal accent is one of our favorite finishes.

We list some of our favorite hardware and other suppliers at the back of the book in the Resources and Acknowledgments sections.

Hardware and closures. Clockwise from upper left: snaps, zippers, grommet and snap pliers, slides and D-rings, magnetic snaps, swivel hooks, flip and press locks, grommets and eyelets, turn and pivot locks, additional hooks and closures and hand-sew snaps.

Backbone Techniques

A main *Sew4Home* goal is to create "light-bulb moments" with detailed instructions that allow you to finally understand how to successfully complete all the steps in a project. Our biggest thrill is when we hear someone say, "You make me feel like I really can do it."

Key to this are the techniques that make up the projects, from sewing specialty seams, to making a boxed corner that forms the bottom of a bag, to inserting a zipper. Refer to the articles listed in the Resources section at the end of this book for many of our most popular step-by-step technique tutorials, or simply visit us at sew4home.com to browse all the options.

When starting out, read through a project several times. We call this, "making it in your head." It's a much better process than simply plunging in and hoping for the best.

If a particular step or series of steps seems troublesome, try making a prototype from scrap fabric. Sometimes a process simply doesn't sink in until you try it a few times. Doing this on scraps gives you confidence, so when you step up to the final fabric, you're a practiced pro!

Finally, don't beat yourself up if something goes wrong. Mistakes happen to the best of us. *Anyone* who sews understands that some seams just weren't meant to be. The good news: Ripping out a seam and starting over is something we all do. With a little care and patience, it's usually an easy fix, and no one but you will likely know it happened. It's better to start over if your first attempt fails. You'll *always* be happier in the end.

Color and Design

There are entire books on this topic, so we're giving you only the big themes to keep in mind when putting together a color palette and fabric mix for your project.

Start with a basic color scheme. Decide whether you want warm undertones (reds, pinks, yellows, oranges), cool (blues, greens) or neutrals (off-whites, tans, grays). Within those tones, consider whether you want them to be vivid and energetic, pale and serene, or dark and intense. Although not always true, too vivid can look garish, too pale can appear stark or washed out, and too dark may feel somber.

With your color scheme in mind, turn next to color balance. Choose a primary color, secondary color and accent color. To achieve the most visually pleasing composition, keep the balance of color at roughly 60% primary, 25–30% secondary and 10–15% accent.

Experiment with fabric. We mix standard quilting cottons with canvas, faux leather and fur, wool and more. Texture, color and weight all work together to create the most professional looks.

Think about proportion, style and scale. It's better to use varying amounts of each fabric within a project. In other words, three equal-size pieces of fabric are not as appealing as a dominant or primary fabric combined with a smaller cut of a secondary fabric and then just a small accent amount of the third. Even if you only use two different fabrics, avoid using the same amount of each. In addition, stay away from the same-size print motif from one fabric to the next. Stir it up with some large prints, medium prints and smaller prints. Scale creates drama and interest in your finished piece. If all of the patterns are the same scale, the result can be lifeless.

Finally, consider adding in some texture. Mixing textures is not difficult, but use restraint. A texture is most appreciated when it's not competing with too many other textures.

Color Block Tote

Big, bold blocks of color and texture create a stunning out-and-about tote. It finishes at a generous size, so you can load it up with a day's shopping treasures or your knitting, sewing and crafting supplies. We used a classic black patent leather vinyl in combination with a rich faux leather in an alligator grain. The longer handles let you carry it by hand or over your shoulder.

Finished Size

About 13" wide × 15" high × 5" deep (33cm × 38cm × 12.5cm)

Sewing Tools

Clips to hold layers together (instead of pins)

Walking or even-feed foot

Nonstick presser foot, optional

General supplies listed on pages 8–10

Materials

½ yard (45.5cm) midweight vinyl or faux leather, 54"+ (137cm+) wide, for bag top exterior and handles

¼ yard (23cm) midweight vinyl or faux leather, 54"+ (137cm+) wide, for bag bottom exterior

¾ yard (68.5cm) quilting-weight fabric for bag lining

¾ yard (68.5cm) medium-weight fusible interfacing

All-purpose thread to match fabric

Wax or parchment paper, if you do not have a nonstick presser foot

Project Notes

- You need exactly 45" (114.5cm) in width for the bag lining; if you are concerned about the exactness of your cutting skills, purchase a full yard (91.5cm).

- Measurements are given as width × height.

Getting Started

1. From the fabric for the bag top exterior and handles, cut the following:

    -   2 strips 25" × 2½" (63.5cm × 6.5cm) for the straps
    -   2 rectangles 14" × 11" (35.5cm × 28cm) for the main front and back panels
    -   2 rectangles 6" × 11" (15cm × 28cm) for the side panels

2. From the fabric for the bag bottom exterior, cut the following:

    -   2 rectangles 14" × 8½" (35.5cm × 21.5cm) for the bottom front and back panels
    -   2 rectangles 6" × 8½" (15cm × 21.5cm) for the bottom side panels

3. From the fabric for the bag lining, cut the following:

    -   2 rectangles 19" × 18½" (48.5cm × 47cm)
    -   1 rectangle 7" × 11" (18cm × 28cm) for the pocket

4. From the fusible interfacing, cut the following:

    -   2 rectangles 14" × 11" (35.5cm × 28cm)
    -   2 rectangles 6" × 11" (15cm × 28cm)
    -   2 rectangles 14" × 8½" (35.5cm × 21.5cm)
    -   2 rectangles 6" × 8½" (15cm × 21.5cm)

Fuse the Interfacing

1. Following the manufacturer's instructions, fuse a piece of interfacing to the wrong side of each corresponding exterior panel.

Note: You may have been cautioned against using fusible interfacing with faux leathers and vinyls. However, if you are careful, it can be done. You don't want your iron on its highest heat, but if you use a pressing cloth, you can adhere the interfacing to each of the pieces without any issues.

Construct the Upper and Bottom Portions

1. Find the four upper panels (the faux alligator panels in our sample). Align one side panel, right sides together, with the front panel.

2. Clip in place, if need be; however, many faux leathers and vinyls stick to themselves, so you may not need any additional help to keep the layers in place.

3. Thread the machine with thread to match the upper panels in the top and bobbin.

4. Using a ½" (1.3cm) seam allowance, stitch the two panels together (Figure 1). We used a walking foot for the entire construction of the bag. This is optional.

5. Repeat Step 4 to sew the remaining side panel to the opposite side of the front panel.

6. Align the back panel, right sides together, with the remaining raw edge of the right side panel. Stitch in place, still using a ½" (1.3cm) seam allowance. Leave the final seam unsewn at this point, giving you a long strip rather than a tube.

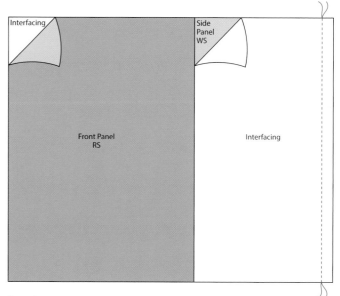

Figure 1

7. Grade the seams, which means to cut one side of the seam allowance narrower than the other to reduce bulk. Press the seams toward the center panels.

Note: Remember to use a pressing cloth when pressing faux leather.

8. Place a piece of wax or parchment paper on top of the faux leather. You need just a thin strip the length of the panel. This will help a standard presser foot move across the faux leather.

9. Topstitch the length of each seam to hold that pressed seam allowance in place. Your topstitched seam should be about ¼" (6mm) from your original seam (Figure 2).

Note: If you have access to a nonstick presser foot, you can skip the paper layer and stitch directly across the faux leather.

10. If using paper, when done, simply tear away the paper strip from the finished seam.

11. When your three seams are topstitched, place the remaining raw edges together to form a tube. Using a ½" (1.3cm) seam allowance, stitch this seam as you did the others. Then turn the tube right-side out and topstitch this final seam (Figure 3).

Note: When you topstitch this seam, you'll notice the faux leather may not be super pliable; you'll need to futz with it a bit to get it to lay flat under the needle. This is why we stitched the other three seams with the faux leather flat.

Figure 2

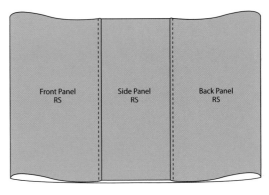

Figure 3

Topstitching and Edgestitching

Topstitching is a line of stitching that adds detail to seams and edges and is meant to be visible from the right side of the project. The stitching is usually more than ⅛" (3mm) from the edge or seam and can be done as a straight stitch, decorative stitch or with multiple rows of stitching. It can feature a thread color that allows the stitching to blend in or stand out as a decorative element.

Edgestitching is usually less than ⅛" (3mm) from the edge or seam. It is traditionally, but not always, a straight stitch in a color that blends into the fabric.

For the best look, we recommending lengthening your stitch for both topstitching and edgestitching.

12. Rethread the machine with thread to match the bottom panels in the top and bobbin.

13. Repeat the above steps to construct the bottom part of the bag in the black vinyl.

14. Clip the panels together (Figure 4).

15. Stitch, turn, topstitch and remove any protective paper.

Assemble the Top and Bottom Portions

1. One of the beauties of this bag is how perfectly the seams match. When you have strong color blocks like this, rather than busy prints, the accuracy of your seams is very important. Place the upper and bottom tubes right sides together. Match up all four seams exactly. Clip the layers together (Figure 5).

2. Using a ½" (1.3cm) seam allowance, stitch the two tubes together all the way around.

3. Using a pressing cloth, press the seam allowance *down* toward the bottom panels.

4. Before you turn the bag right-side out to topstitch, grade the seam allowance as you did above.

5. Turn the bag right-side out, and with the machine still threaded with thread to match the bottom bag panels, topstitch the seam allowance in place within the bottom panel (Figure 6).

6. As above, place parchment paper down or use a nonstick presser foot and stitch about ¼" (6mm) from the original seam. If your machine has a free arm, now is a good time to use it. You can also cuff the top of the bag to allow it to better fit through the machine.

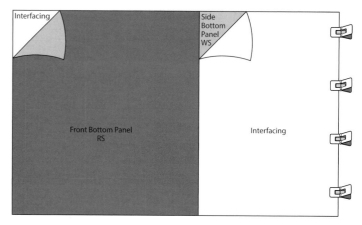

Figure 4

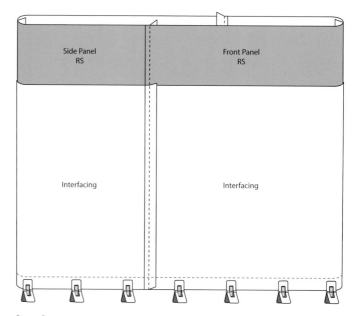

Figure 5

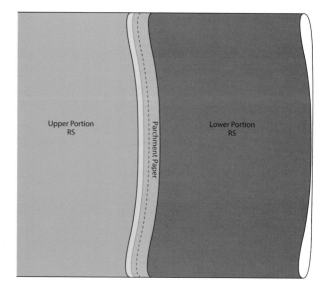

Figure 6

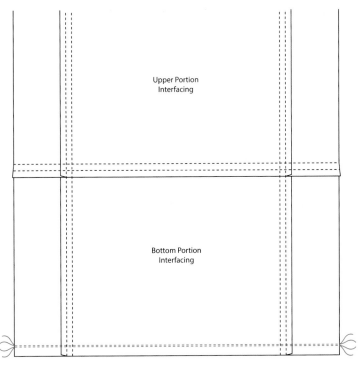

Upper Portion
Interfacing

Bottom Portion
Interfacing

Figure 7

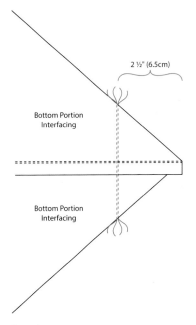

2 ½" (6.5cm)

Bottom Portion
Interfacing

Bottom Portion
Interfacing

Figure 8

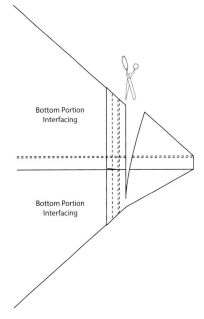

Bottom Portion
Interfacing

Bottom Portion
Interfacing

Figure 9

7. Turn the bag inside out. Carefully align the seams and flatten the bag in order to sew the bottom seam. Clip in place.

8. Using a ½" (1.3cm) seam allowance, sew across the bottom of the bag. Stitch across again to reinforce the seam (Figure 7).

9. With the sewn fabric still right sides together, using both hands, pinch and pull apart the corner. As you pull, the fabric will begin to make a little peak with the corner point at the top and the seam lines running down the middle of the front and the back. Match these side and bottom seams. Place a pin in the seams to hold them together. It is very important that you exactly match the seams; that is what will make the lines of your finished corner look good.

10. Our bag is designed to have 5" (12.5cm) sides and base. To create this width, your boxed corner seam needs to be half that finished width, or 2½" (6.5cm) from the tip of each corner peak. Draw a line at this mark and stitch twice for reinforcement (Figure 8).

11. Trim back each "peak" to about ¼" (6mm) from the seam lines (Figure 9).

Note: Faux leather will not ravel, so it's not necessary to finish this trimmed seam allowance. If you are working with a fabric prone to fraying, finish the seam allowance with a zigzag or similar overcasting stitch.

12. Turn the main bag right-side out and push out the corners.

Create the Lining and Its Pocket

1. Find the 7" × 11" (18cm × 28cm) pocket piece. Fold this piece in half right sides together so it is now 7" × 5½" (18cm × 14cm).

2. Using a ½" (1.3cm) seam allowance, stitch along both sides and across the bottom, pivoting at the corners. Leave about a 2"–3" (5cm–7.5cm) opening along the bottom for turning.

3. Clip corners and press open the seam allowances (Figure 10).

4. Turn right-side out. Push out the corners so they are nice and sharp. A chopstick or long knitting needle works well for this.

5. Fold in the raw edges of the opening so they are flush with the sewn seam. Press flat.

6. Pin the pocket in place on one 19" × 18½" (48.5cm × 47cm) lining piece. The pocket should be centered side to side and 5" (12.5cm) down from the top raw edge.

7. Edgestitch the pocket in place along both sides and across the bottom, pivoting at the corners and with a generous backstitch at the beginning and end of the seam, i.e., at the pocket top (Figure 11). This is a stress point for the pocket, and it's smart to secure the seam well.

8. Place the lining piece with the sewn pocket and the second lining piece right sides together, aligning all raw edges. Pin in place along both sides and across the bottom.

9. Leave an 8"–10" (20.5cm–25.5cm) opening along the bottom. You'll use this opening at the end to turn the finished bag right-side out.

10. Using a ½" (1.3cm) seam allowance, stitch both sides and across the bottom, pivoting at the corners. Remember to lock your stitch on either side of the opening (Figure 12). If your machine doesn't have a lock stitch feature, simply pull the thread ends to the back of the piece and knot the threads to secure the stitches.

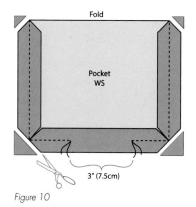

Figure 10

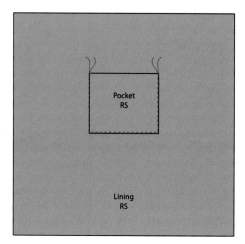

Figure 11

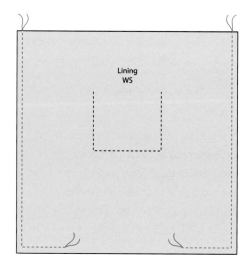

Figure 12

11. With the lining still wrong-side out, box the bottom corners following the same steps as above for the exterior of the bag.

Create the Bag Handles

1. Find the two 25" × 2½" (63.5cm × 6.5cm) handle strips. Lay them right-side down and flat on your work surface.

2. With a ruler and fabric pencil, measure 1" (2.5cm) in from the right side and draw a line all the way from one end to the other. Then measure ½" (1.3cm) in from the left side and draw a second line from one end to the other (Figure 13).

3. Fold in the right side along the drawn line. Finger press in place.

4. Fold in the left side along the drawn line, overlapping the first fold, as if you were folding a letter to mail. Finger press in place. Clip in place (Figure 14).

5. Repeat steps 2–4 to fold and clip the remaining strap.

6. Cut a strip(s) of wax or parchment paper the length of the strap. Place the paper *under* one handle, positioning the handle strap with the fold facing up.

7. Place the handle and paper under the presser foot; the paper will be against your machine's feed dogs.

Note: If you are not using a walking or even-feed foot, you may also want to place a layer of wax or parchment paper on top, between the faux leather and the presser foot.

8. Sew down the middle of the strap, staying close to the cut edge (Figure 15).

Note: There's no need for any additional finish on this cut edge. It will not ravel or fray because it is faux leather (or vinyl). If you take a look at some of the purses in your closet, you may see this exact same finish. It's quite standard on leather and vinyl because it is very hard (if not darn near impossible) to turn a leather or vinyl tube right-side out—it will stick to itself!

Figure 13

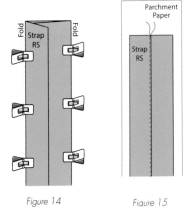

Figure 14

Figure 15

9. With the bag body right-side out, measure 2½" (6.5cm) in toward the center from each side seam along the top raw edge. Do this on both the front and the back panel. Mark these four points with a clip.

10. Place one handle on the front and one on the back, aligning one raw handle end at each clip point. The right side of the handle should be against the right side of the bag. This means the handle seam will be facing up. You can align the handle seam with each clip point. Edgestitch each handle in place (Figure 16).

Attach the Lining

1. With the exterior bag right-side out and the lining wrong-side out, slip the lining over the exterior so the two are right sides together. Align the bottom corners and clip around the top raw edges (Figure 17).

2. Using a ½" (1.3cm) seam allowance, stitch the exterior bag to the lining around the top opening.

3. Press the lining seam allowance down.

4. Pull the faux leather bag through that 8"–10" (20.5cm–25.5cm) opening you remembered to leave in the bottom of the lining (Figure 18).

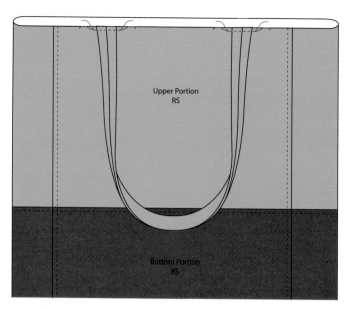

Figure 16

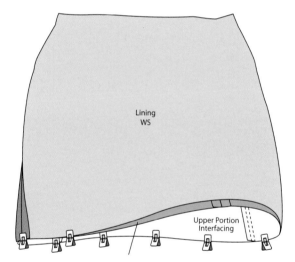

Figure 17

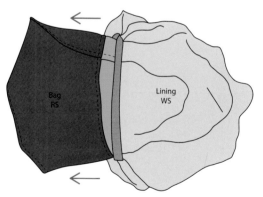

Figure 18

5. Press the opening in the lining flat so the raw edges are flush with the sewn seam. Pin and edgestitch closed (Figure 19).

6. Push the lining down into position inside the bag. Topstitch around the entire top edge of the bag to finish (Figure 20).

Note: We did not use wax paper for this final topstitching because the lining was against the machine's feed dogs. Going slowly, the upper feed dogs in the walking foot were able to move easily across the faux leather. If you are not using a walking foot, you may want to add a layer of wax or parchment paper between the presser foot and the fabric.

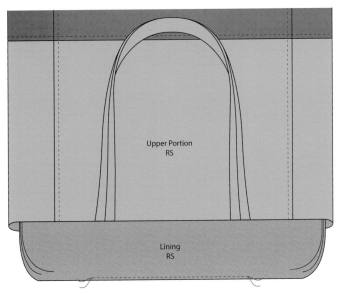

Figure 19

Figure 20

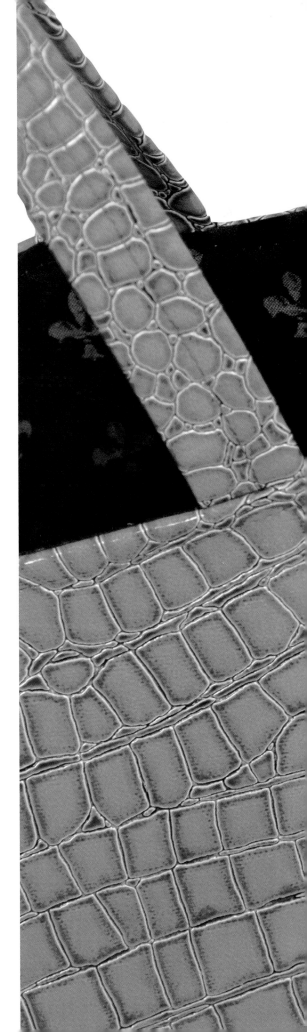

Easy Wave-Top Shoulder Bag

This bag is beginner friendly but has a great finished look! And we show you exactly how to make that pretty curving top. Our clever stitch-and-turn method means zero raw edges without having to create a separate lining. The shoulder strap is soft cotton webbing, super simple and a perfect match for this tall, slim bag. Go with a bold exterior print that shouts out your style.

Finished Size

About 11" wide × 14" high × 2" deep (28cm × 35.5cm × 5cm)

Sewing Tools

General supplies listed on pages 8–10

Materials

¾ yard (68.5cm) midweight cotton for the bag exterior and the lining pockets

½ yard (45.5cm) standard-weight cotton or similar for the bag lining

½ yard (45.5cm) fusible batting

1¼ yards (1.1m) strapping material, 1½"– 2" (3.8cm–5cm) wide

All-purpose thread to match fabrics and strap

Grid or pattern paper to create the top curve (at least a 14" × 17" [35.5cm × 43cm] rectangle)

Project Notes

- You could use soft cotton web-bing (our choice for this sample) for the strap, make your own strap from coordinating fabric or use leather or suede.

- Measurements are given as width × height.

Getting Started

1. From the fabric for the bag exterior and pockets, cut the following:

   - 1 rectangle 12" × 32" (30.5cm × 81.5cm)
   - 1 square 8" × 8" (20.5cm × 20.5cm)
   - 1 square 5" × 5" (12.5cm × 12.5cm)

2. From the fabric for the bag lining, cut 1 rectangle 12" × 32" (30.5cm × 81.5cm).

3. From the fusible batting, cut 1 rectangle 12" × 32" (30.5cm × 81.5cm).

4. From your grid or pattern paper, cut 1 rectangle 14" × 17" (35.5cm × 43cm).

5. Following our 1" (2.5cm) grid in Figure 1, draw a cresting wave curve to become the top of the bag. We also drew lines down either side about 5" (12.5cm) to make it extra easy to align the template.

Note: You could draw a free-form curve. Don't be scared; there's no wrong way to do it.

6. Cut the curve along your drawn line.

Fuse the Batting

1. Place the fusible batting against the wrong side of the exterior rectangle. Following the manufacturer's instructions, fuse the batting in place (Figure 2).

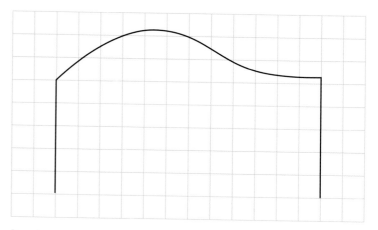

Figure 1

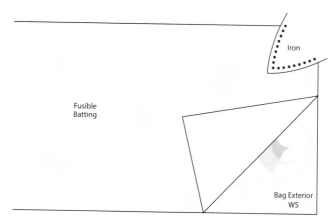

Fusible
Batting

Iron

Bag Exterior
WS

Figure 2

Cut the Top Curves

1. Place the lining rectangle and the exterior/batting rectangle right sides together, aligning the raw edges all around.

2. Pin your curve template in place on one end of the assembled layers. Align the side edges and bring the curve very close to the raw edges (Figure 3). Pin and carefully cut.

3. Flip the template and cut the opposite end (Figure 4).

Note: You need to flip the template so the curves are cut in the same relative position and will match up when you fold the bag to stitch the sides.

Create and Place the Pockets

1. Find the 8" × 8" (20.5cm × 20.5cm) interior pocket piece. If you're working with a directional fabric, make sure you orient the piece on your work surface so the design is running the right way. Fold back the raw edges ½" (1.3cm) on both sides and the bottom. Press well.

2. Along the top raw edge, fold back ½" (1.3cm) and press, then fold an additional 1" (2.5cm) and press again (Figure 5).

3. Stitch close to the folded edge to create a simple hem along the top of the pocket.

4. Repeat Steps 1–3 with the 5" × 5" (12.5cm × 12.5cm) interior pocket piece.

5. Find your curved lining piece. Place it right-side up and flat on your work surface.

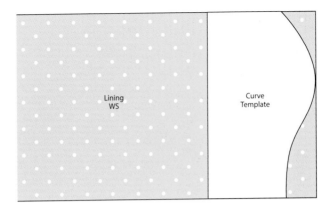

Figure 3

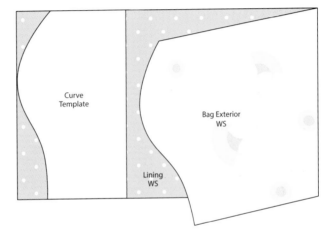

Figure 4

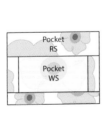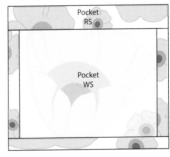

Figure 5

6. Separate the lining panel and place it right-side up and flat on your work surface. Place each pocket 5" (12.5cm) down from the top of the curve and centered side to side. On the large pocket, this should be about 2⅝" (6.7cm) from each side. On the small pocket, this should be about 4" (10cm) from each side (Figure 6). Pin in place. The top hem of each pocket should be facing the curve.

7. Edgestitch each pocket in place along both sides and across the bottom, pivoting at the corners (Figure 7).

Create the Bag Body

1. Place the exterior and lining right sides together, carefully aligning the raw edges all the way around and sandwiching the pockets between the layers. Pin in place, leaving a 5"–6" (12.5cm–15cm) opening along one side (Figure 8).

2. Using a ½" (1.3cm) seam allowance, stitch around all sides of the layered fabrics. Go slowly around the curved ends, stopping as needed, with your needle in the down position, to slightly adjust your presser-foot position. Remember to lock stitch at either side of the side opening.

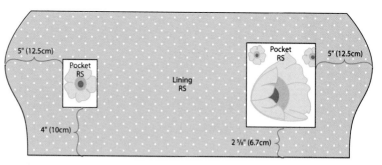

Figure 6

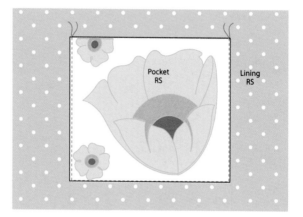

Figure 7

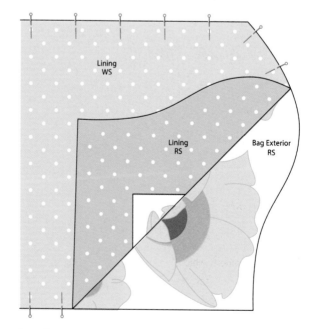

Figure 8

3. Trim the seam allowance to ¼" (6mm) and clip the curves (see sidebar). Do not trim back the seam allowance along the opening (Figure 9).

4. Turn right-side out through the opening. Use your finger or a long, blunt tool, such as a chopstick or knitting needle, to help smooth out the curved ends.

5. Fold in the raw edges of the opening so they are flush with the sewn seam. Pin in place.

Note: At this point, we added a *Sew4Home* label to the front of the bag. If you'd like to add your personal label, position it in the bottom right corner at least 1½" (3.8cm) in from the side and up from the bottom to account for the boxed corner.

6. Fold the bag in half, right sides together. Make sure the layers are smooth and flat across the bottom fold. Align the top curves so they are a perfect match. Pin both sides.

7. Using a ⅜" (1cm) seam allowance, stitch both sides from bottom to top (Figure 10).

8. With the bag still wrong-side out, the next step is to box the bottom corners of the bag. Using both hands, pinch and pull apart the bottom corner. As you pull, the fabric will begin to make a little peak with the corner point at the top and the seam line running down the middle of one side.

9. Center the side seam within this triangle peak.

10. Mark for 2" (5cm) box corners, which means your "box" will be half that size, or 1" (2.5cm) from the triangle peak.

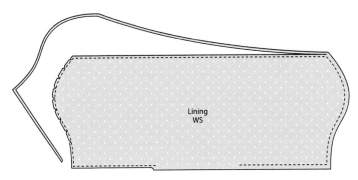

Figure 9

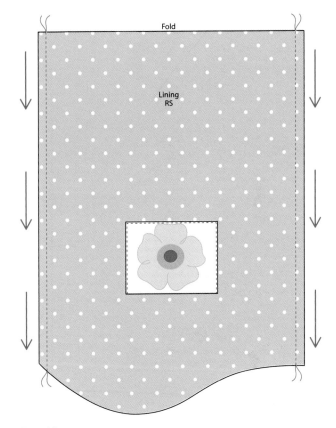

Figure 10

Clipping Curves

Clip notches of excess fabric from the seam allowance so when the piece is turned right side out, the fabric won't bunch up along the outward curve's pretty shape. Space the notches ½" (1.3cm) apart and be sure not to clip the seam.

Box Stitch

A box stitch, which is simply a square or rectangle with an *X* in it, provides a high level of strength and stability to a strap, and when done with precision, it also adds a pretty detail.

11. Stitch back and forth along the marked line two or three times to reinforce (Figure 11).

Note: Do *not* trim away the peak on either side. There are no raw edges, so we are going to simply leave the little peaks as is—they'll be hidden inside the bag.

Attach the Strap

1. Prepare your strap as needed. If you are making a strap from fabric scraps, fold and stitch a narrow strip to make a long tube. If you are using cotton webbing, suede or leather, these fabrics won't fray, so there's no need to finish the edges; you're good to go at a width of about 1½"–2" (3.8cm–5cm).

2. Cut your strap to a length of about 45" (114.5cm). Pin it in place at this length, and if possible, try it on the intended user. Adjust it slightly longer or shorter to best fit.

3. Fold under one end about ¾" (2cm) and pin in place at the top of one side seam. Center the folded end across the seam. The bottom folded edge sits 2¾" (7cm) down from the top finished edge (Figure 12).

4. Draw in a horizontal stitching line, or place a marking pin as shown below, about ¼" (6mm) from the top finished edge of the bag.

5. Inside the bag, spread the finished seam allowance wide open so it lays as flat as possible.

6. Box stitch in place (Figure 13). You'll need to maneuver the bag carefully under the presser foot to keep everything flat. Don't be afraid to twist and fold the body of the bag to get it to lay right; you can press it when you're done.

7. Repeat Steps 3–6 to attach the other end of the strap. Remember to keep the inside seam nice and flat prior to box stitching.

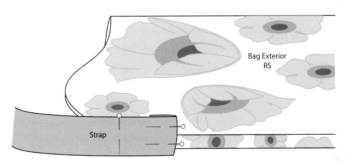

Figure 12

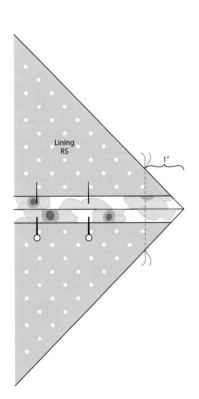

Figure 11

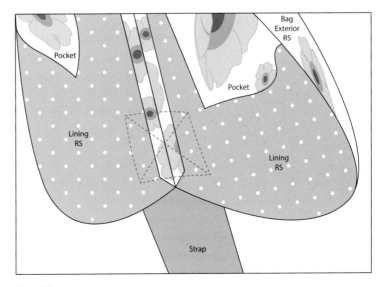

Figure 13

Fold-Over Zippered Clutch

Two colors, two fabrics, one sleek and elegant bag that's ready for an evening out. Discover how easy it is to insert a top zipper between exterior and lining layers. We also explain how to add zipper tabs. Use this technique to get a perfect fit within an opening every time. Mix fabric textures for a sophisticated look; we combined a hand-dyed ikat linen with copper faux leather.

Finished Size

About 15" wide × 11" high (38cm × 28cm) flat; about 15" wide × 7" high (38cm × 18cm) folded

Sewing Tools

Clips for use with the faux leather, optional

Zipper foot

Quarter-inch seam foot, optional

Walking or even-feed foot, optional

Nonstick foot, optional

General supplies listed on pages 8–10

Materials

½ yard (45.5cm) medium-weight cotton sateen, blended linen or similar for the exterior top

⅓ yard (30.5cm) light- to medium-weight faux leather or similar, 54"+ (137cm+) wide, for the exterior base

½ yard (45.5cm) lightweight polyester for the lining

½ yard (45.5cm) low-loft fusible fleece for the lining

1 metal zipper, 14" (35.5cm)

All-purpose thread to match fabric

Project Notes

- Yardage for the exterior top allows for fussy cutting either a horizontal or vertical cut.

- Measurements are given as width × height.

Getting Started

1. From the fabric for the exterior top, fussy cut 2 rectangles 16½" × 6½" (42cm ×16.5cm).

2. From the fabric for the exterior bottom, zipper tabs and zipper pull, cut the following:
   - 2 rectangles 16½" × 6½" (42cm × 16.5cm)
   - 2 rectangles 1¼" × 2½" (3.2cm × 6.5cm) for the zipper tabs
   - 2 strips ⅛" × 13" (3mm × 33cm) for the zipper pull

3. From the fabric for the lining, cut 2 rectangles 16½" × 12" (42cm × 30.5cm).

4. From the fusible fleece, cut 2 rectangles 16½" × 11½" (42cm × 29cm).

Prepare the Exterior Panels

1. Find the four exterior panels (two tops and two bottoms). Match up each top with a bottom.

Note: If your top and/or bottom print is directional, make sure you align the bottom of the top panel and top of the bottom panel.

2. Place the panels right sides together, aligning one 16½" (42cm) side for each pair. Pin in place.

3. Using a ½" (1.3cm) seam allowance, stitch across the panels (Figure 1).

4. Press the seam allowance down toward the faux leather panel.

Note: Remember, when pressing faux leather, reduce your heat, press from the wrong side only and use a pressing cloth.

5. Flip over both sewn exterior panels to the right side.

6. Thread your machine with thread to match the faux leather in the top and bobbin. Topstitch within the faux leather panel along the horizontal seam, staying very close to the original seam (Figure 2). Lengthen the stitch for the best look. We used 3.0mm. Topstitch both panels in the same manner.

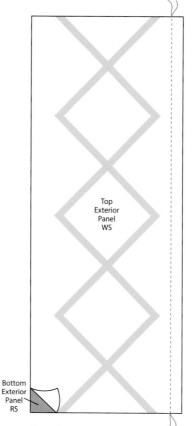

Figure 1

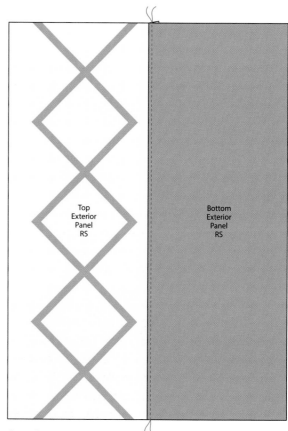

Figure 2

Note: If you have any trouble moving across the faux leather with your standard presser foot, try a walking foot or a nonstick foot, or insert a strip of wax or parchment paper between the foot and the faux leather. We used a walking foot.

7. Find the two 16½" × 11½" (42cm × 29cm) pieces of fusible fleece. Following the manufacturer's instructions, fuse the fleece to the wrong side of each sewn exterior panel. The fleece should align with the sides and the bottom of the exterior panel, but should sit ½" (1.3cm) down from the top edge of the panel (Figure 3).

Note: Traditional wisdom advises you to not use fusible products on faux leather. However, we tested the idea and researched others online who had done the same and decided we could buck tradition with a bit of caution. Lower the heat setting on your iron (try the wool setting) and reduce the pressure when you move from the top fabric to the faux leather. A little steam can also help it adhere.

8. Set the exterior panels aside.

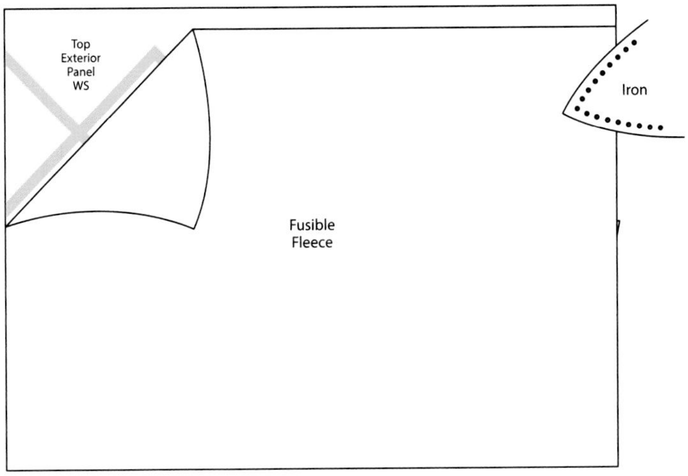

Attach the Zipper

1. Find the 14" (35.5cm) zipper and the two 1¼" × 2½" (3.2cm × 6.5cm) tabs. Place one tab on each end of the zipper, right sides together with the raw ends flush. Pin in place.

Note: We based the width of these tabs on our zipper. Cut your tab as needed to best fit your zipper; you want the tab to fit within the zipper tape.

2. Return the stitch length to normal. Stitch the zipper tabs in place, running your seam just below the top and bottom zipper stops (Figure 4).

3. Finger press the zipper tabs away from the zipper on each end.

4. Find the front and back exterior panels. Place the finished front panel of the bag right-side up on your work surface.

Note: The front and back panels are essentially the same. However, if you feel one pair looks better than the other, then that should be the front.

Figure 3

Top Exterior Panel WS

Iron

Fusible Fleece

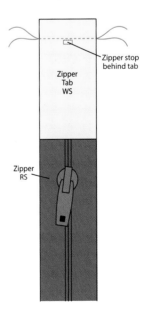

Zipper stop behind tab

Zipper Tab WS

Zipper RS

Figure 4

5. Lay your zipper upside down along the top edge of the front panel (i.e., right sides together with the zipper teeth facing down against the right side of the fabric). The edge of the zipper tape should be even with the fabric's raw horizontal edge. Make sure the zipper is centered between the left and right sides of the panel. The zipper tabs may extend beyond the raw edges of the panel a bit (Figure 5).

6. Pin the zipper to the panel, being careful to pin through just the top of the zipper. You need to be able to open and close the zipper; you can't do that if you've pinned through the whole thing.

7. Open the zipper a little bit.

8. Attach a zipper foot. If your machine allows adjustment of the needle position, move your needle to its left-most position.

9. Stitch as close to the zipper as the foot will allow, removing the pins as you sew (Figure 6).

10. Go slowly. When you get to where you can start to feel you're approaching the zipper pull, stop with your needle in the down position.

11. Twist your fabric around slightly and carefully close the zipper. Reposition your fabric and finish sewing to the end. Be very careful and go slowly; you want your seam line to be super-duper straight.

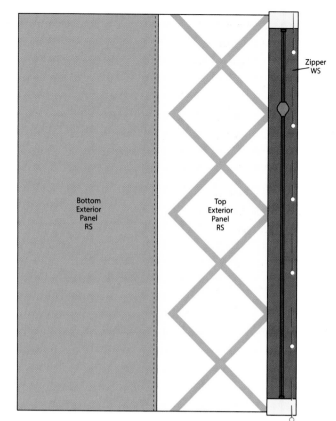

Figure 5

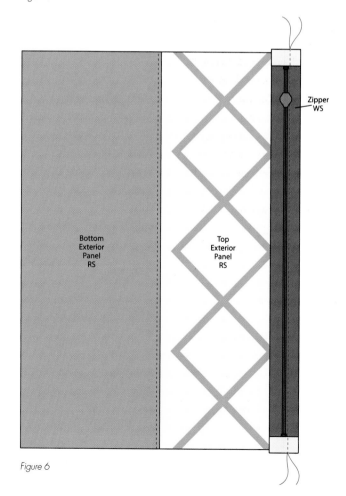

Figure 6

12. Press the panel away from the zip-per. The zipper should be standing up from the panel with the remaining raw edge exposed (Figure 7).

13. Repeat Steps 5–11 to attach the remaining raw edge of the zipper to the other exterior panel.

14. Take care to keep your seam allow-ance the same on both sides so the zipper teeth are nicely centered.

15. You now have panels stitched in place on either side of the zipper, and the excess width is neatly filled in with the pretty faux leather zipper tabs.

16. If necessary, rethread your machine with thread to match the upper fabric in the top and bobbin.

17. Switch back to your regular presser foot or a quarter-inch seam foot (that's what we used). Lengthen the stitch as above for the front panel. Topstitch along each side of the zipper, run-ning your stitching as close to the edge of the fabric as possible. As above with the zipper insertion, to get close enough to the zipper with your topstitching, you will need to open and close the zipper to work around the pull (Figure 8).

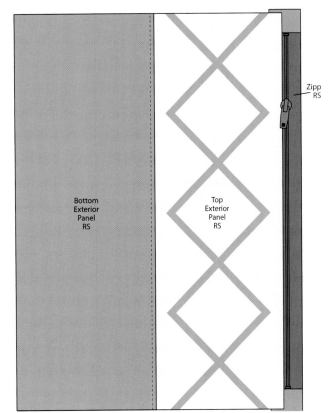

Figure 7

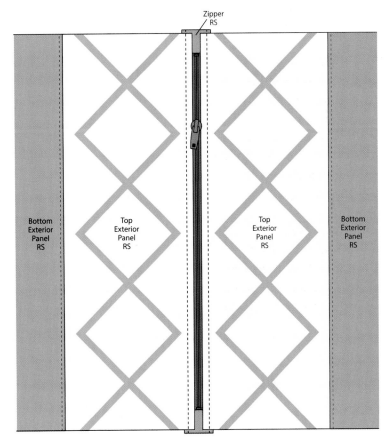

Figure 8

Complete the Exterior Bag

1. Make sure the zipper is open at least halfway. Fold the two panels right sides together, aligning the raw edges along both sides and across the bottom and making sure the horizontal seams match up. Pin in place.

2. Return the stitch length to normal. Using a ½" (1.3cm) seam allowance, stitch along both sides and across the bottom, pivoting at the bottom corners (Figure 9). Use a substantial backstitch at both the beginning and end of your seam to reinforce these stress points at either end of the zipper.

Note: We switched back to a walking foot. When you are sewing together two different types of fabrics, such as the faux leather and linen we used for our sample, the layers are more likely to stretch and shift against one another. The built-in feed dogs of a walking foot work in combination with the machine's feed dogs to provide extra control.

3. Clip the corners at a diagonal and trim away any excess zipper-tab fabric. We also trimmed the fleece from the seam allowance. At the edge of the fabric, it's relatively easy to gently break the bond to the fusible fleece to allow the trimming.

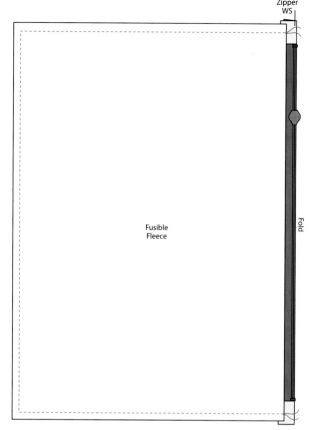

Figure 9

4. Finally, at the very top of each seam, make a small snip in the zipper tab to free the seam allowance so you can press it open (Figure 10).

Note: Leave the finished exterior bag wrong-side out.

Create and Insert the Lining

1. Find the two 16½" × 12" (42cm × 30.5cm) lining pieces. Place the two pieces right sides together, aligning all the raw edges. Pin in place along both sides and across the bottom.

2. Using a ½" (1.3cm) seam allowance, stitch along both sides and across the bottom, pivoting at the corners.

3. Clip the corners at a diagonal, press open the seam allowance and turn the lining right-side out. Gently push out the corners so they are nice and square. Press flat on low heat.

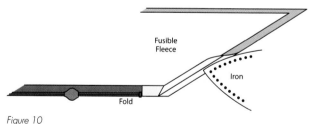

Figure 10

4. Fold down the top raw edge of the lining ½" (1.3cm) all the way around (Figure 11). Press well.

5. Find the exterior bag. It should still be wrong-side out. With the lining right-side out, slip the exterior bag inside the lining so the two bags are now wrong sides together.

6. Align the bottom and side seams. The top folded edge of the lining should fall below the zipper teeth by about ⅛" (3mm). If it doesn't, adjust the fold to fit and gently re-press.

7. Pin the layers together.

8. Thread a hand-sewing needle with thread to match the lining.

9. Hand stitch the lining to the bag, using very small stitches (Figure 12). Stitch along the front and the back, but leave the lining loose where it wraps over the side seams. This allows some give in the lining so it folds smoothly as you zip the bag open and shut.

10. Gently turn the bag right-side out through the zipper opening. Push the corners out so they are as smooth as possible and press the bag flat. Make sure you cover the faux leather with a pressing cloth and use a low heat setting.

11. Find the two thin faux leather strips. Place them one on top of the other and fold in half. The ends should be flush.

12. Push the middle fold through the hole in the zipper pull, creating a loop. Slip the ends through the loop and pull down gently to secure (Figure 13). This is just like how you'd attach a gift or price tag.

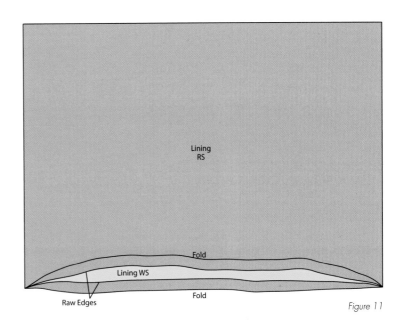

Figure 11

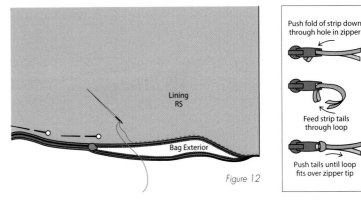

Figure 12

Push fold of strip down through hole in zipper

Feed strip tails through loop

Push tails until loop fits over zipper tip

Figure 13

Kid's Vintage Book Bag

This shape, size and style falls into the "satchel" classification, which means even its category is retro cool! Step through some of the best bag features, such as a full front flap, with ease. Then tackle your fear of hardware; we explain grommets, D-rings, twist locks and more! Think kids have all the fun? We show you how to lengthen the strap to upsize this cute bag for your very own.

Finished Size

About 10" wide × 7½" high × 2½" deep (25.5cm × 19cm × 6.5cm) with 30" (76cm) strap. Increase the strap length to about 43" (109cm) for an adult.

Sewing Tools

Zipper foot

Walking or even-feed foot

General supplies listed on pages 8–10

Materials

½ yard (45.5cm) medium-weight duck, canvas or similar fabric for the bag and flap exterior

½ yard (45.5cm) medium-weight duck, canvas or similar fabric for the flap lining, lining pocket and straps

⅛ yard (11.5cm) medium-weight duck, canvas or similar fabric for the side gusset

½ yard (45.5cm) quilting-weight cotton for the bag lining

¾ yard (68.5cm) heavy batting or foam interfacing, 20"+ (51cm+) wide

Scrap or ¼ yard (23cm) medium-weight fusible interfacing, 18" (45.5cm) wide, for the lining pocket, optional for the strap

1 turn-lock purse closure, 1¼" (3.2cm)

2 metal eyelets/grommets, ⁷⁄₁₆" (1.1cm)

2 D-rings, ¾" (2cm)

2½ yards (2.3m) packaged piping in a color to accent the exterior fabric

All-purpose thread to match fabric

Wax or parchment paper for pattern; you want the paper to be semi-transparent

Small cup or glass about 3½" (9cm) in diameter to round corners of pattern

Project Notes

- To give the bag the proper stand-up-on-its-own stability and form, we recommend the foam over batting. It's very easy to sew and provides great body.

- Measurements are given as width × height.

Getting Started

1. From the wax or parchment paper, cut the following:

   - 1 rectangle 11" × 8½" (28cm × 21.5cm) for the bag body
   - 1 square 10" × 10" (25.5cm × 25.5cm) for the flap

2. Using the cup or glass as a template, round the two bottom corners of each pattern piece (Figure 1).

3. From the fabric for the bag and flap exterior, fussy cut one flap using the flap pattern.

Note: We took the time to carefully cut the exterior pieces so the car motif aligned from the flap to the front of the bag. The main thing to keep in mind is that the flap attaches at the back about 1½" (3.8cm) down from the top raw edge of the exterior panel.

4. Pin the body pattern piece underneath the actual cut flap fabric panel. The top of the flap should be about 1½" (3.8cm) above the top of the pattern piece. Pin the two layers together.

5. Move the pinned layers to the front exterior panel fabric and adjust until you get a motif match (Figure 2).

6. When the match is set, remove the flap and cut out the front exterior panel.

7. Use this front exterior panel to cut one matching back exterior panel.

8. From the fabric for the flap lining, lining pocket and straps, fussy cut the following:

   - Using the flap pattern, cut 1

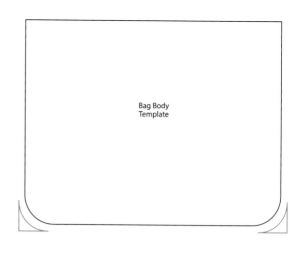

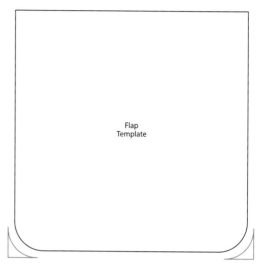

Figure 1

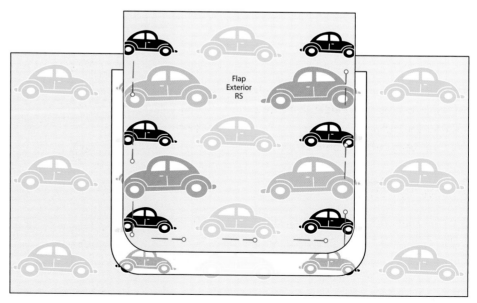

Figure 2

Note: If using a directional fabric as we did, remember that the exterior of the flap is cut right-side up but the lining of the flap is cut upside down (Figure 3). This way, when the flap is lifted up to open, its motif will appear right-side up.

- 1 rectangle 6½" × 9" (16.5cm × 23cm) for the lining pocket
- 1 strip 2" × 41") (5cm × 104cm) for the strap. Then subcut the strip into one 27" (68.5cm) length and one 14" (35.5cm) length.

Note: For an adult strap, cut 1 strip 2" × 55" (5cm × 139.5cm), then subcut the strip into one 41" (104cm) length and one 14" (35.5cm) length. If your fabric is not wide enough for a 55" (139.5cm) single cut, cut two strips and seam them together.

9. From the fabric for the side gusset, cut 1 strip 3" × 26½" (7.5cm × 67.5cm).

Note: We cut 1 strip 3" × WOF (7.5cm × WOF), and then subcut to 26½" (67.5cm) to get the best fussy cut. Our WOF was 45" (114.5cm).

10. From the fabric for the lining, cut the following:

- Using the bag body pattern, cut 2
- 1 strip 3" × 26½" (7.5cm × 67.5cm) for the side gusset

11. From the foam (or fleece), cut the following:

- Using the bag body pattern, cut 2
- Using the flap pattern, cut 1
- 1 strip 3" × 26½" (7.5cm × 67.5cm) for the side gusset

Note: The side panels are all cut long to allow extra to work with to get a smooth curve. It will be trimmed to fit flush after it's sewn in place.

12. From the interfacing, cut 1 rectangle 6½" × 4½" (16.5cm × 11.5cm) for the pocket.

Note: We did not use interfacing for our strap, but you could certainly add it for a more structured finish. You need a 2" × 41" (5cm × 104cm) strip. If choosing this option, fuse the interfacing in place prior to subcutting the strap into two lengths.

Create the Flap

1. Find the exterior flap panel and the piping. Pin the piping to the right side of the flap around the outer perimeter, leaving the top straight edge plain. Clip the piping to ease it around the bottom rounded corners.

2. Attach a zipper foot. Baste the piping in place (Figure 4).

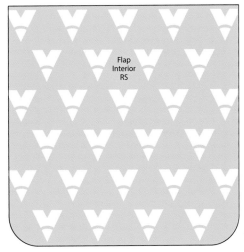

Figure 3

Figure 4

3. Start and end the basting seam just shy of the top edge of the fabric. At each end of the piping, use a seam ripper to open the bias tape and clip back the piping cord about ½" (1.3cm) (Figure 5). This will allow a flat end for a smooth finish along the top of the flap.

4. Refold the piping into position and finish the basting seam.

5. Collect the other flap pieces: the lining and the foam. Layer these three pieces: foam, flap lining right-side up, exterior flap (with the piping in place) right-side down. Pin in place all the way around, leaving a 3"–4" (7.5cm–10cm) gap for turning along the top straight edge. You'll stitch with the exterior flap on top so you can follow along in the piping's basting seam.

6. Still using a zipper foot, stitch all the way around with about a ½" (1.3cm) seam allowance (Figure 6). We say about because your goal should actually be to stitch along the piping's basting seam, which may or may not be exactly ½" (1.3cm).

7. Clip the curves and trim back the foam (or batting) to the seam line to reduce bulk.

8. Turn the flap right-side out through the top opening. Push out the corners so they are nicely rounded. A long, blunt tool, such as a knitting needle or chopstick, works great for this. Fold in the raw edges of the top opening ½" (1.3cm) so they are flush with the sewn seam and pin closed (Figure 7).

9. Press the flap from both the front and back. Set the flap aside.

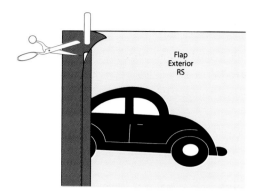

Figure 5

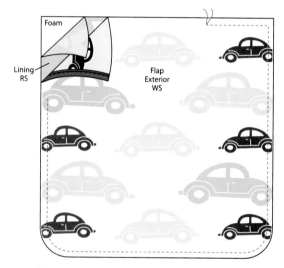

Figure 6

Figure 7

Create the Exterior

1. Find the front and back exterior panels and the remaining piping. Pin the piping around the outer edge of both pieces. The top edges remain plain.

2. As above with the flap, use a zipper foot to baste the piping in place.

3. Also as above, remember to clip about ½" (1.3cm) from each end of the piping to allow a flat start and finish (Figure 8).

Figure 8

4. With the piping basted in place, find the side gusset and the three remaining foam panels. Place a foam panel against the wrong side of each exterior piece and the side gusset.

5. On the two exterior panels, machine baste the foam to the fabric, following along the piping's basting seam. Then trim back the foam to the basting line. Do not baste the side gusset.

Note: Foam batting is also available as a fusible product, which would allow you to adhere it to the panels with heat and skip the basting steps.

6. Place the back panel right-side up/foam-side down on your work surface. Place the flap right-side up in position on the back panel. The flap should be centered side to side, and the top straight edge of the flap should sit parallel to and 1½" (3.8cm) down from the top raw edge of the back panel. Pin the flap in place across the top straight edge.

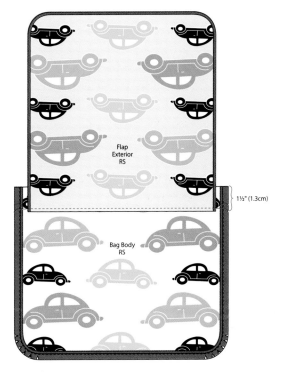

Figure 9

Note: At this point, you'll notice the cars are opposite one another on the two panels. This is correct. When the flap comes down over the top, everyone will be going the right way.

7. Switch to a walking or even-feed foot if possible, and make sure the machine is threaded with thread to best match the exterior fabric in the top and bobbin. Lengthen the stitch (we recommend about 3.0mm).

8. Edgestitch across the top straight edge of the flap through all the layers (Figure 9). Start and stop your seam at the side of the flap; do not stitch onto the exterior panel.

9. Insert the latch half (the opening) of the turn lock at the center bottom of the flap. It should be centered side to side, and the center of the opening should be 1" (2.5cm) up from the bottom finished edge of the flap (Figure 10). Position and trace the inside oval and the circles for the screws.

10. Enlarge the oval to include the screw circles and carefully cut this shape through all the layers. This oval shape should be slightly smaller than the overall size of the latch half itself.

11. Insert the hardware following the manufacturer's instructions. See the Resources on page 124 for information on additional technique tutorials, including one on hardware installation.

12. Find the side gusset/foam. Pin the layers together: starting at one corner, and with right sides together, pin one edge of the gusset to the back exterior panel. The piping is sandwiched between the layers. As mentioned above, the gusset is a bit longer than necessary so you have extra with which to work to ease around the corner. This means your opposite end will extend beyond the top of the panel.

13. Using a ½" (1.3cm) seam allowance, stitch the gusset in place against the back panel (Figure 11). We switched back to a zipper foot, moved the needle to the left and followed along in the previous line of basting stitching.

Figure 10

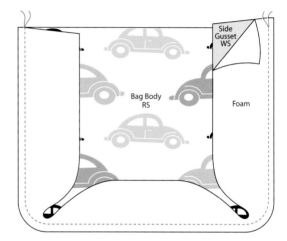

Figure 11

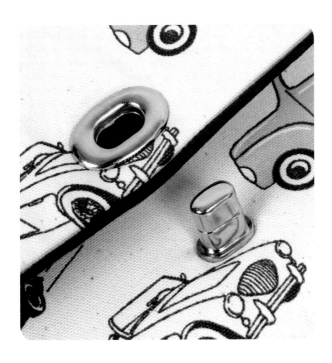

14. You now have one free edge of the side gusset remaining.

15. Pin this free edge to the front exterior panel, right sides together (Figure 12). Make sure the flap is up and out of the way.

16. Using a ½" (1.3cm) seam allowance, stitch in place. Clip all the curves. Trim away the excess side gusset fabric/foam.

17. The top edges of the sides, front and back should now be even all the way around (Figure 13).

18. To reduce the bulk around the top edge of the bag, machine baste through both layers ¾" (2cm) from the raw edges all the way around.

19. Trim back the foam to the basting seam line as you did above with the exterior panels.

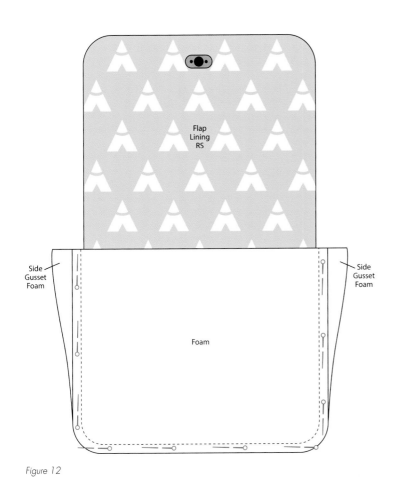

Figure 12

Figure 13

20. After trimming, fold back the top raw edge of the fabric, which will roll the basting seam toward the inside where it will be hidden. Pin the fold in place all the way around (Figure 14).

21. Place the remaining half of the turn lock in place. Fold the flap down into position to double-check the fit. You don't want the flap to pull or pinch across the top opening; it should be an easy fold-over. Our measurements fell at about 5½"–5¾" (14cm–14.5cm) down from the top folded edge, 1¾" (4.5cm) up from the bottom piping and centered side to side (Figure 15).

Note: Your exact position may vary based on the fabric and interfacing you choose, so we strongly recommend doing your own test rather than relying solely on our measurements.

22. Insert the lock hardware following the manufacturer's instructions.

23. Set aside the completed exterior.

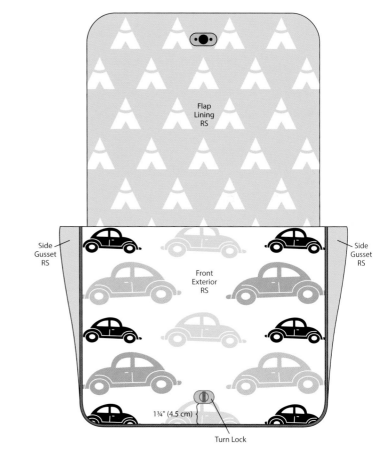

Figure 15

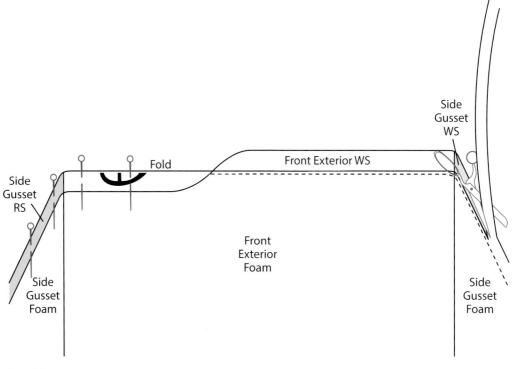

Figure 14

Create the Lining

1. Find the 6½" × 9" (16.5cm × 23cm) lining pocket panel and the 6½" × 4½" (16.5cm × 11.5cm) interfacing panel. Following the manufacturer's instructions, fuse the interfacing to one half of the pocket panel on the wrong side.

2. Fold the pocket in half, right sides together, so it now measures 6½" × 4½" (16.5cm × 11.5cm).

3. Pin in place along both sides and across the bottom. Leave about a 3" (7.5cm) opening along the bottom for turning.

4. Using a ½" (1.3cm) seam allowance, stitch along both sides and across the bottom, pivoting at the corners. Lock your seam on either side of the 3" (7.5cm) opening (Figure 16).

5. Clip the corners and press open the seam allowance.

6. Turn the pocket right-side out through the opening. Gently poke out the corners so they are nice and sharp. Press flat, pressing in the raw edges of the opening so they are flush with the sewn seam.

7. Find one of the two lining panels. Place the pocket on the right side of the panel. The pocket should be positioned 2½" (6.5cm) down from the upper raw edge of the panel and centered side to side.

8. Edgestitch the pocket in place along both sides and across the bottom, pivoting at the corners (Figure 17). This closes the opening in the seam. For the cleanest finish, use a lock stitch to start and end your seam or leave your thread tails long and hand knot to secure.

9. Following the same steps as above for the exterior, pin the side gusset to the lining panel with the pocket. Clip the corners of the gusset to ease around the curve.

10. Stitch in place, using a ½" (1.3cm) seam allowance (Figure 18).

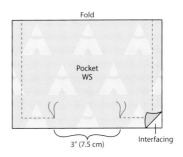

Figure 16

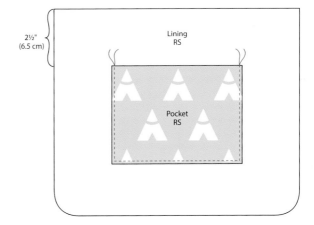

Figure 17

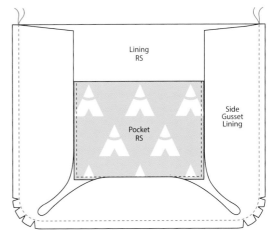

Figure 18

11. Repeat to add the remaining lining panel to the free raw edge of the gusset.

12. Trim away the excess side gusset fabric as above.

13. Press back the top edge of the lining ½" (1.3cm) all the way around.

Assemble the Exterior and Lining and Insert the Grommets

1. Find the exterior bag. It should be right-side out. Find the lining bag. It should be wrong-side out. Slip the lining bag inside the exterior bag so the two bags are now wrong sides together. Align the side seams. The pocket should sit against the back of the bag.

2. The top folded edge of the lining should sit just below (about ¹⁄₁₆" [2mm] below) the top folded edge of the exterior bag. If it does not align as described, refold one or both edges to get the best even, yet slightly offset, alignment all the way around.

3. Pin the lining to the exterior all the way around the top.

4. Fold the flap down and out of the way.

5. If necessary, rethread the machine with thread to match the exterior bag and lining. We stitched with the lining facing up, so we used thread to match the lining in the top and the exterior in the bobbin.

6. Edgestitch around the top, through all the layers (Figure 19). We recommend a walking foot since you are stitching through several layers plus the thick foam.

7. Measure 1½" (3.8cm) down from the top seamed edge at each side seam. This is where the center hole of the grommet should hit at each side. Mark each grommet hole (Figure 20).

8. Cut the holes for both grommets through all the layers.

9. Following the manufacturer's instructions, insert each grommet.

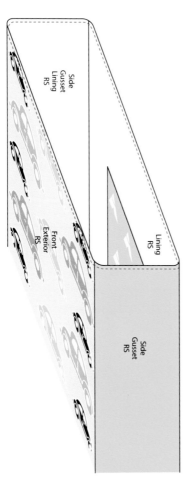

Figure 19

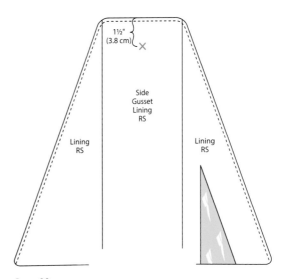

Figure 20

Create and Attach the Strap

1. Find the two strap pieces. On each strap, press back one long raw edge ½" (1.3cm).

2. Press back the opposite long raw edge ¼" (6mm).

3. Press back both 2" (5cm) ends ½" (1.3cm) (Figure 21).

4. Lap the ¼" (6mm) folded edge over the ½" (1.3cm) folded edge and press flat, forming a ⅝" (1.5cm) wide strap (with an offset lap) that is finished on all sides. Repeat for second length of strap.

5. Topstitch down the long lapped edge and across both ends (Figure 22).

6. Loop one end of the shorter strap through the right grommet from front to back. Bring the end through and pin it against itself. The lapped side of the strap is considered the back.

7. Stitch across to secure this looped end in place (Figure 23). The opposite end remains free.

8. Repeat to loop one end of the longer strap through the left grommet. If using a directional fabric as we did, insert the proper end so the motifs on both straps match up.

9. Insert the opposite end of the longer strap through the two D-rings. Be careful to make sure there are no twists or turns in your strap. The end looped through the D-rings should be against the back of the strap, exactly as is the end through the grommet. Remember, the lapped side of the strap is considered the back.

10. Stitch across to secure this end in place, running the seam as close as possible to the D-rings (Figure 24).

11. Slip the short end through the double D-rings and adjust to fit.

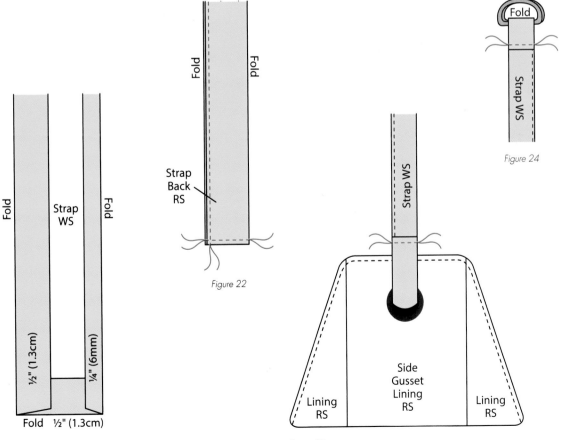

Figure 21

Figure 22

Figure 23

Figure 24

Yoga Mat Sling Tote

Keep fit, be fashionable. Ribbons accent this bright and beautiful yoga sling. Branch out and learn tips for working with these jacquard ribbons as well as specialty fabrics, like this tote's heavyweight PUL (polyurethane laminate). The double-drawstring design lets you slide your mat in or out from either end. And a handy zippered outside pocket holds extra necessities.

It is designed for a standard $24\frac{1}{3}$" wide × 5" diameter (61.8cm × 12.5cm) mat.

Finished Size

About 28" long × 6" in diameter when gathered closed at each end

Sewing Tools

Denim or jeans needle, size no. 14 to no. 16

Nonstick presser foot

Clear-view foot, optional

Zipper foot

Quarter-inch seam foot

General supplies listed on pages 8–10

Materials

2 yards (1.8m) ribbon, $1\frac{1}{2}$" (3.8cm) wide

$3\frac{1}{2}$ yards (3.2m) ribbon, $\frac{7}{8}$" (2.2cm) wide

$\frac{3}{4}$ yard (68.5cm) medium-weight polyurethane laminate (PUL) or athletic nylon, 54"+ (137cm+) wide, for the bag body, pocket and strap

$1\frac{1}{4}$ yards (1.1m) round cord elastic (sometimes called shock cord), $\frac{1}{8}$" (3mm)

1 plastic zipper, 4" (10cm)

2 eyelets, $\frac{1}{4}$" (6mm) for the drawstring channels

2 eyelets, $\frac{5}{32}$" (4mm) for the bottom air-release holes

2 double cord stops for the $\frac{1}{8}$" (3mm) cord

2 small beads for the drawstring pulls, optional

All-purpose thread to match fabric

All-purpose thread to match ribbon and/or invisible thread in clear

Project Notes

- The denim or jeans needle works best when sewing the ribbon and nylon fabric combination to avoid skipped stitches.

- For the ribbon, we used and recommend a vibrant jacquard.

- The beads are optional; they simply give you something to grip when pulling the drawstring. The hole in the beads should be large enough to fit the stretchy cord, and the bead color should match the cord. We used black pony beads.

- For this project, we prefer invisible thread for stitching the ribbon.

- Measurements are given as width × height.

Getting Started

1. From the main fabric, cut the following:

   - 1 panel 34" × 20" (86.5cm × 51cm) for the main bag body
   - 1 strip 2¾" × 29" (7cm × 73.5cm) for the bag strap
   - 2 rectangles 5" × 8" (12.5cm × 20.5cm) for the pocket

2. Cut the 1½" (3.8cm) ribbon into 2 lengths of 20" (51cm) and 1 length of 29" (73.5cm).

3. Cut the ⅞" (2.2cm) ribbon into 6 lengths of 20" (51cm).

4. Cut the cord elastic into 2 lengths of 22" (56cm).

Create the Strap

1. Thread your machine with thread to match the main fabric in the top and bobbin.

2. Find the 2¾" × 29" (7cm × 73.5cm) strap piece. Place it wrong-side up on your work surface. Using your ruler, measure 1" (2.5cm) in from each 29" (73.5cm) raw edge, and draw two parallel lines the length of the strip.

3. Fold in each raw edge to its nearest drawn line. Machine baste both folds in place (Figure 1).

Note: This type of fabric doesn't press well, so it's harder to get it to hold a folded measurement. Basting in place produces the same result.

4. Find the 29" (73.5cm) length of wide ribbon. Center the ribbon along the strip, concealing the fabric's raw edges beneath the ribbon. Pin in place.

5. Rethread your machine with clear thread in the top and bobbin (or thread to match the ribbon in the top and to match the fabric in the bobbin). Edgestitch along both sides of the ribbon (Figure 2).

6. Remove the basting stitches and set the strap aside.

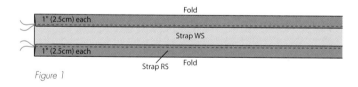

Figure 1

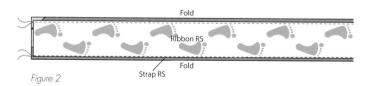

Figure 2

Attach the Ribbons to the Body

1. Place the bag body panel right-side up and flat on your work surface. Using a clear ruler, measure 4" (10cm) in from one raw side edge (one 20" [51cm] edge). This will be the placement line for the first ribbon. You can either draw a guideline with your fabric pen or pencil or simply use your ruler as your guide.

2. Find one 20" (51cm) length of narrow ribbon. Place it along the 4" (10cm) guideline. Pin in place.

Note: If you'd rather not use pins to hold your ribbons in place, you can keep them from shifting by applying a little basting glue or strips of lightweight fusible web to the wrong side of the ribbon lengths.

3. Edgestitch in place along both sides of the length of ribbon (Figure 3).

4. Find a second length of the narrow ribbon. Place this length ⅛" (3mm) from the first ribbon. Pin or fuse in place.

Note: If your ribbon is directional, make sure each ribbon is oriented the right way prior to stitching in place.

5. Edgestitch in place along both sides of the length of ribbon.

6. Find a 20" (51cm) length of wide ribbon. Place it ⅛" (3mm) from the second narrow ribbon. Pin or fuse in place (Figure 4).

7. Edgestitch in place along both sides of the length of ribbon.

8. Turn the fabric panel to build the ribbon stack along the opposite side. Repeat the same placement pattern on this opposite side of the bag. Then add two additional lengths of the narrow ribbon, placing them with the same ⅛" (3mm) spacing.

9. Edgestitch in place along both sides of all the ribbons (Figure 5).

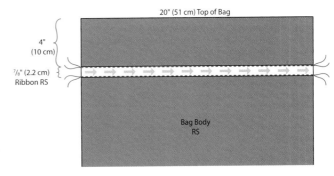

Figure 3

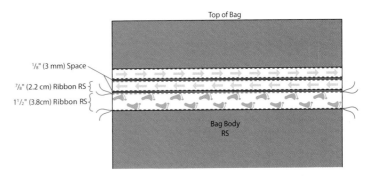

Figure 4

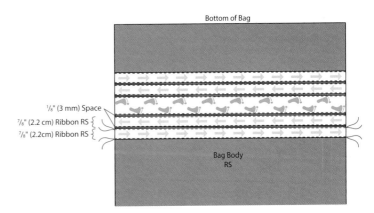

Figure 5

10. When finished, you should have three ribbons (two narrow and one wide) on one side of the bag body panel (this will become the top of the bag) and five ribbons (four narrow and one wide) on the opposite side of the bag body panel (this will become the bottom of the bag).

Create the Zippered Pocket

1. Rethread the machine with thread to match the fabric in the top and bobbin.

2. Find one 5" × 8" (12.5cm × 20.5cm) pocket panel and the zipper.

3. Place the main bag body panel right-side up on your work surface. Measure to find the center of the top 20" (51cm) side (the three-ribbon side). Place your ruler along the centerline.

4. Fold the pocket panel in half wrong sides together (so it is now 2½" × 8" [6.5cm × 20.5cm]). Place the fold along the ruler at the centerline. The top edge of the pocket should be 1" (2.5cm) from the third sewn ribbon. Pin one edge of the pocket in place (the bottom layer of the fold) (Figure 6).

5. Remove the ruler and unfold the pocket panel and pin the rest of the pocket in place. The pocket should be right-side down.

6. With a fabric pen or pencil, draw a 4" × ⅜" (10cm × 1cm) box. Center this narrow box side to side on the pocket panel and place it 1" (2.5cm) down from the upper edge (Figure 7).

7. Adjust your stitch length to about 1.8mm. This tighter stitch will make the corners of the box sharper and stronger. Stitch along the drawn box.

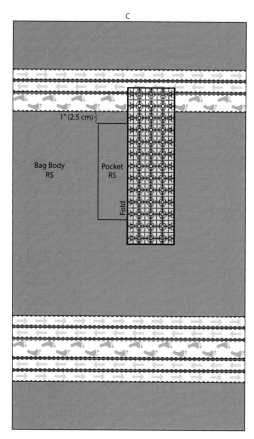

Figure 6

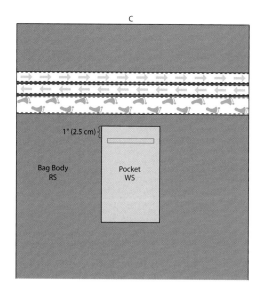

Figure 7

8. Cut through the center of the box, then clip into each corner (Figure 8). You are cutting through both layers. Be careful not to cut into your stitching.

9. Turn the pocket right-side out, bringing it through the opening to the back of the bag (Figure 9).

10. Smooth out the corners of the box and pin flat. Normally you would just press the box flat, but with nylon fabric, you need to pin it.

11. Place the opening over the zipper, centering the zipper teeth. Pin in place.

12. Attach a zipper foot. Reset the machine to a standard stitch length (about 2.4mm). Edgestitch the zipper in place (Figure 10).

13. Go around all four sides, opening and closing the zipper as necessary to keep the zipper pull out of the way of the needle.

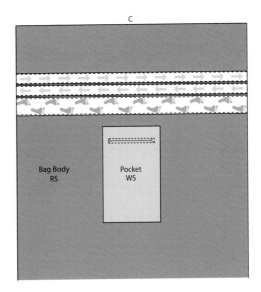

Figure 8

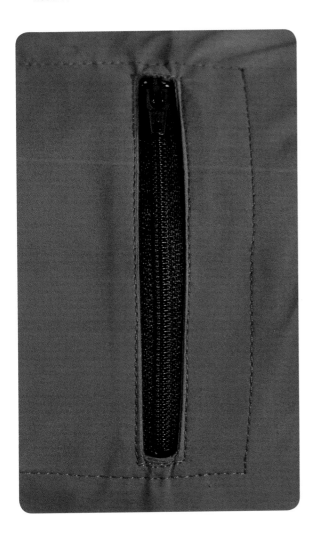

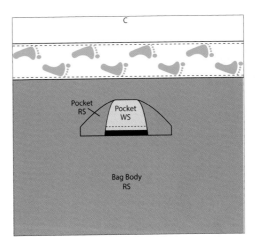

Figure 9

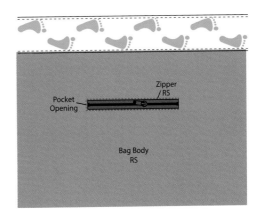

Figure 10

14. When the zipper is sewn in place, flip the bag body panel to the wrong side.

15. Find the remaining 5" × 8" (12.5cm × 20.5cm) pocket panel. This is the pocket lining. Place it right-side down directly on top of the sewn pocket panel so all edges of both panels are flush. Pin in place through all the layers (Figure 11).

16. Flip the bag body panel to the right side. Edgestitch around all four outer edges of the pocket through all three layers (Figure 12). Remember to pivot at each corner.

Note: The pocket is thick enough that you should be able to simply follow the edge with your presser foot, feeling through the fabric. If you are uncertain about your ability to keep your stitching accurate and straight, measure and draw in guidelines to follow (with an erasable fabric pen). Or, when pinning, you can insert your pin points an exact ¼" (6mm) in from the raw edge. When flipped to the right side, follow the pins as a guideline.

Create the Drawstring Channels

1. On both raw side edges of the main panel (the 20" [51cm] sides), fold back the edge ¼" (6mm) and machine baste this narrow hem in place (Figure 13). You can measure, pin and stitch or simply use a quarter-inch seam foot, which was our choice.

Note: As above with the strap, this basting step is a replacement for pressing.

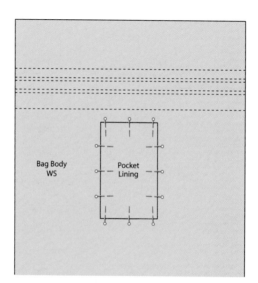

Figure 11

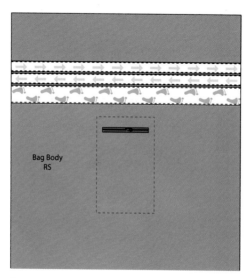

Figure 12

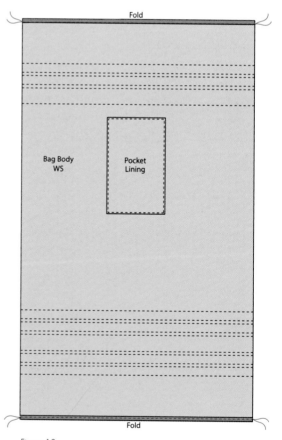

Figure 13

2. Flip the panel to the right side. Find the exact center of this newly hemmed side. Measure 1" (2.5cm) from the finished edge and mark the placement for the ¼" (6mm) eyelet.

3. Insert the eyelet following the manufacturer's instructions (Figure 14).

4. Fold back the finished side edge ¾" (2cm) and pin in place.

5. Edgestitch in place, staying as close as possible to the inner folded edge, to create the drawstring channel (Figure 15). Go slowly and be careful to avoid the outer edge of the eyelet.

6. Repeat steps 2–5 to create the drawstring channel on the opposite side.

Add Toggles

1. Find the two beads, the two lengths of shock cord and the two toggles. Squeeze the toggle so the holes line up, then slip one length of cord through one hole. Pull it through and slip on a bead.

2. Thread the end of the cord through the second hole of the toggle (remember to squeeze first to align the holes). Continue to pull the cord through so it extends evenly from both sides with the bead at the center.

3. Slip both ends of the cord through one eyelet, feeding one end through the channel in one direction and the other end in the other direction (Figure 16). The cord is thick enough to easily work it through the channel without a safety pin.

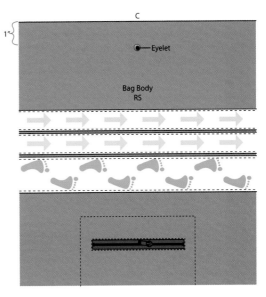

Figure 14

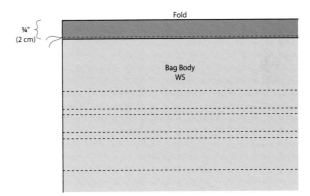

Figure 15

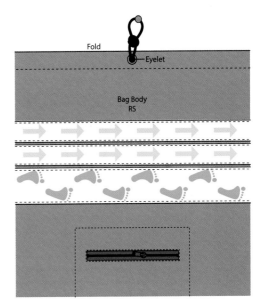

Figure 16

4. Pull each end of the cord through so it just barely extends out of the end of the channel on both sides. Pin in place.

5. Machine baste across each end to hold the cord in place during the remaining construction (Figure 17).

6. Repeat Steps 1–5 to attach the toggle and cord to the opposite side.

Assemble the Bag and Add Air Holes

1. Place the bag body panel right-side up on your work surface.

2. Find the finished strap. Place the strap right-side down (ribbon-side down) along the upper raw edge of the bag body panel. Align the 1½" (3.8cm) ribbon on the strap with the 1½" (3.8cm) ribbons on the bag at both the top and bottom of the bag panel. The raw ends of the strap should be flush with the raw edge of the fabric panel. Pin in place, making sure the strap is not twisted along its length (Figure 18).

3. Pin the strap ends in place. You can machine baste in place for extra security.

4. Fold the completed bag body panel in half, aligning the long raw sides and sandwiching the strap between the layers. Carefully align all the ribbons.

5. Pin in place along the length of the panel.

6. Stitch in place using a ½" (1.3cm) seam allowance (Figure 19).

7. Turn the bag right-side out.

8. At the bottom end (the five-ribbon end), add the two small eyelets to either side of the seam. Mark the position for each eyelet ¼" (6mm) out from the bag center seam line and ¼" (6mm) from the casing seam.

9. Insert each eyelet (Figure 20). These help release air, allowing the yoga mat to easily slide into the bag.

10. Cinch up the bottom end, drop in your mat, cinch up the top end and proceed to class.

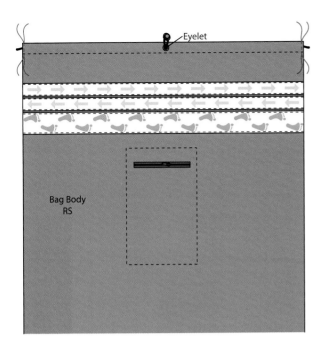

Eyelet

Bag Body
RS

Figure 17

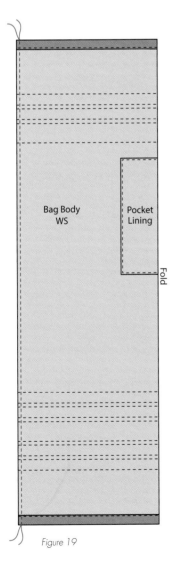

Bag Body
WS

Pocket
Lining

Fold

Figure 19

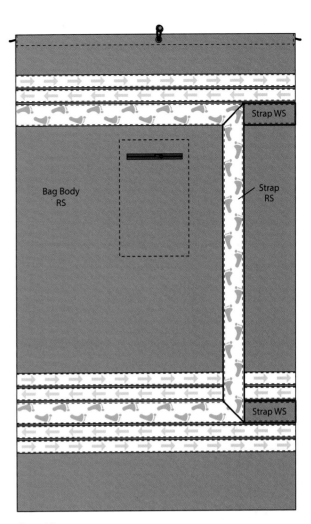

Bag Body
RS

Strap WS

Strap
RS

Strap WS

Figure 18

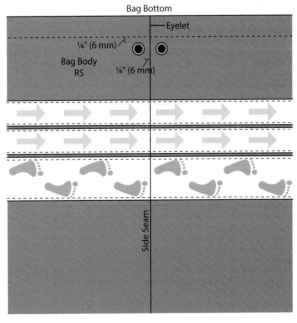

Bag Bottom

Eyelet

¼" (6 mm)

Bag Body
RS

¼" (6 mm)

Side Seam

Figure 20

Pleated Slip-Through Bow Clutch

Our pretty pleated band with its splashy bow adds style and sass but also has a job to do. Slip your hand behind the band and grasp the bottom. It's an innovative way to clutch your clutch. Find out how to press in pleats, create a faux knot bow and insert a zipper. Each of these techniques is easier than you might think, and all can be used on so many other projects.

Finished Size

About 9½" wide × 6½" high (24cm × 16.5cm)

Sewing Tools

Zipper foot

General supplies listed on pages 8–10

Materials

1 yard (91.5cm) sateen-weight cotton, 54" (137cm) wide, for the exterior panels, pleated panel and bow

¼ yard (23cm) quilting-weight cotton for lining

⅓ yard (30.5cm) medium-weight fusible interfacing

⅓ yard (30.5cm) low-loft batting, 45" (114.5cm) wide

⅝ yard (57cm) lightweight fusible interfacing, 20" (51cm) wide, for the bow

1 zipper, 7" (18cm)

All-purpose thread to match fabric

Project Notes

- Centering a beautiful motif for the exterior panels as well as the bow will give you a more dramatic look. Extra yardage is included in the quantity for the exterior fabric to accommodate this. If you choose not to fussy cut, you can get away with as little as ½ yard (45.5cm).

- Measurements are given as width × height.

Getting Started

1. From the fabric for the exterior, fussy cut the following:

   - 2 rectangles 10½" × 7½" (26.5cm × 19cm)
   - 1 rectangle 11" × 13" (28cm × 33cm) for the pleated panel
   - 1 rectangle 21" × 10" (53.5cm × 25.5cm) for the bow
   - 1 square 3½" × 3½" (9cm × 9cm) for the bow's faux knot
   - 2 strips 1¼" × 2½" (3.2cm × 6.5cm) for the zipper tabs, fussy cut to match the top of the bag

Note: We cut frames from graph paper that had an open interior area the same size as the main panels. We moved the frames around on the fabric until we found the best areas of the motif to use.

2. From the fabric for the lining, fussy cut 2 rectangles 10½" × 7½" (26.5cm × 19cm).

3. From the *medium-weight* fusible interfacing, cut 2 rectangles 7½" × 10½" (19cm × 26.5cm).

4. From the *lightweight* fusible interfacing, cut the following:

   - 1 rectangle 21" × 10" (53.5cm × 25.5cm)
   - 1 square 3½" × 3½" (9cm × 9cm)

5. From the low-loft batting, cut 2 rectangles 10½" × 7½" (26.5cm × 19cm).

Fuse Interfacing and Add Batting

1. Following the manufacturer's instructions, fuse the medium-weight interfacing to the wrong side of both exterior panels. Fuse the lightweight interfacing to the wrong side of the bow panel and faux knot square.

2. Place the two batting pieces right-side up on your work surface. Place a fused exterior panel right-side up on each piece of batting. Pin lightly or hand baste the fabric and batting together.

Create the Pleated Panel

1. Find the 13" × 11" (33cm × 28cm) panel for the pleated accent band. Fold the panel in half, right sides together, so it now measures 6½" × 11" (16.5cm × 28cm). Pin along the 11" (28cm) edge.

2. Using a ½" (1.3cm) seam allowance, stitch along the 11" (28cm) edge, creating a tube (Figure 1).

3. Turn the tube right-side out. Roll the seam to the center back and press the tube flat.

4. Make three ½" (1.3cm) pleats. The first pleat is 1½" (3.8cm) from the top of the band, the subsequent two pleats are ½" (1.3cm) apart, and the edge of the final pleat is ½" (1.3cm) from the bottom of the band (Figure 2). Pin the pleats in place. Lightly press.

5. The pleats go all the way across the band. Pin at both edges as well as through the middle to secure them.

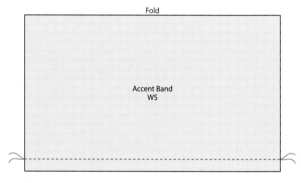

Figure 1

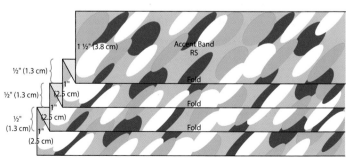

Figure 2

6. Lay the pinned pleated panel at a slight diagonal across the front exterior panel. The left edge should be about 1" (2.5cm) down from the top left corner of the panel; the bottom of the band should be about 1" (2.5cm) up from the bottom right corner of the panel. Pin in place.

7. Machine baste each end of the band in place through all the layers, staying within the seam allowance (Figure 3). The band may extend a bit beyond the panel on each end. Simply trim flush once you've basted the band into place.

Insert the Zipper

1. Find the zipper and the two 2½" × 1¼" (6.5cm × 3.2cm) tabs. Place one tab on each end of the zipper. Place the tab and the zipper right sides together, with the raw ends of each tab about ½" (1.3cm) from the top and ¼" (6mm) from the bottom. You are just covering the top and bottom stops on the zipper. Pin in place.

Note: We based the width of these tabs on our zipper. Cut your tabs as needed to best fit your zipper; you want the tab to fit within the zipper tape.

2. Stitch the zipper tabs in place, running your seam just outside the top and bottom zipper stops (Figure 4).

3. Press the zipper tabs away from the zipper on each end.

4. Find the front and back exterior panels. Place the front exterior panel with its pleated band right-side up on your work surface.

5. Open the zipper about halfway. Lay the zipper right-side down along the top edge of the front panel (i.e., right sides together with the zipper teeth facing down on the right side of the fabric). The horizontal edge of the zipper tape should be flush with the fabric's raw horizontal edge. Make sure the zipper is centered between the left and right sides of the panel. The zipper tabs will extend beyond the raw edges of the panel. They will be trimmed flush later.

Note: You can measure both the panel and the zipper prior to pinning to find the exact center point of each, then match these points.

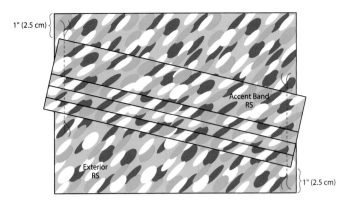

Figure 3

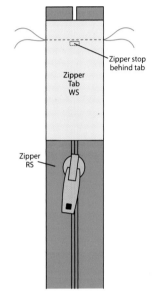

Figure 4

6. Pin the zipper to the panel, being careful to pin through just the top of the zipper. You need to be able to open and close the zipper; you can't do that if you've pinned across the zipper teeth.

7. Attach a zipper foot. If your machine allows adjustment of the needle position, move your needle to its left-most position.

8. Stitch as close to the zipper as the foot will allow, removing the pins as you sew (Figure 5).

9. Go slowly. When you get to where you can start to feel you're approaching the zipper pull, stop with your needle in the down position. Twist your fabric around slightly and carefully close the zipper. Reposition your fabric and finish sewing to the end. Be very careful and go slowly; you want your seam line to be super-duper straight.

10. Press the panel away from the zipper (Figure 6).

11. Repeat steps 5–10 to attach the other side of the zipper to the plain back exterior panel.

12. You now have panels stitched in place on either side of the zipper, and the excess width is neatly filled in with the zipper tabs.

13. Topstitch along each side of the zipper, running your stitching as close to the folded edge of the fabric as possible (Figure 7).

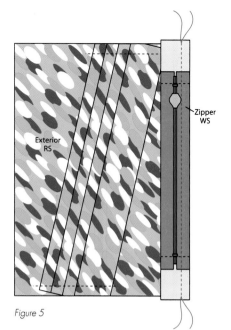

Figure 5

Figure 6

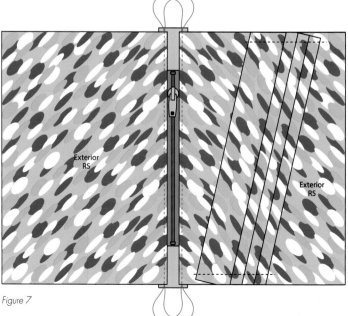

Figure 7

Complete the Exterior

1. Unzip the zipper about halfway again. Fold the two panels right sides together, aligning the raw edges along both sides and across the bottom. Pin in place.

2. Using a ½" (1.3cm) seam allowance, stitch along both sides and across the bottom, pivoting at the bottom corners. Use a substantial backstitch at both the beginning and end of your seam to reinforce these stress points at either end of the zipper.

3. Grade the seam allowance, which means trim the layers of the seam allowance at varying widths. Leave one side of the fabric seam allowance at ½" (1.3cm), trim the batting back to ¼" (6mm), and trim the opposite side of the fabric seam allowance to ⅛" (3mm) (Figure 8).

4. Turn right-side out through the zipper opening and press flat, using a pressing cloth.

Create and Insert the Lining

1. Find the two 10½" × 7½" (26.5cm × 19cm) lining pieces. Place the two lining pieces right sides together. Pin in place along both sides and across the bottom.

2. Using a ½" (1.3cm) seam allowance, stitch along both sides and across the bottom, pivoting at the corners.

3. Clip the corners at a diagonal. Press open the seam allowance (Figure 9).

4. Turn back the top raw edge of the lining ½" (1.3cm) all the way around (Figure 10).

5. Turn the lining right-side out. Gently push out the corners so they are nice and square. Press flat.

6. Find the exterior bag. Turn it wrong-side out. With the lining still right-side out, slip the exterior bag inside the lining so the two bags are now wrong sides together.

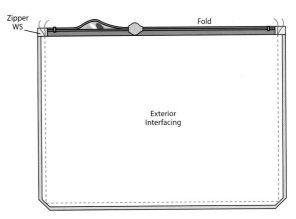
Figure 8

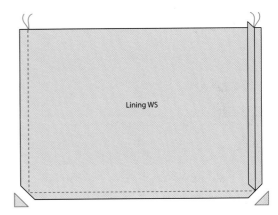
Figure 9

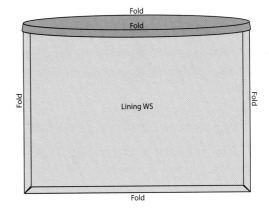
Figure 10

7. Align the bottom and side seams. The top folded edge of the lining should fall below the zipper teeth by about ⅛" (3mm). If it doesn't, adjust the fold to fit and gently re-press.

8. Pin the layers together.

9. Thread a hand-sewing needle. Slip stitch or whipstitch the lining to the bag (Figure 11).

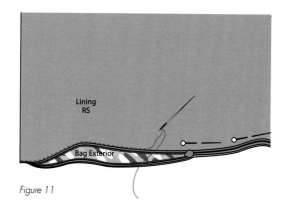

Figure 11

10. Stitch along the front and the back, but leave the lining loose where it wraps over the side seams. This allows some give in the lining so it folds smoothly as you zip the bag open and shut.

11. Turn the finished bag right-side out.

Make and Attach the Bow

1. Find the 21" × 10" (53.5m × 25.5cm) fused rectangle for the bow. Fold it in half so it is now 10½" × 10" (26.5cm × 25.5cm). Pin in place, leaving a 2"–3" (5cm–7.5cm) opening in the center of the seam for turning.

2. Using a ½" (1.3cm) seam allowance, stitch together, creating a tube (Figure 12). Remember to lock your seam on either side of the 2"–3" (5cm–7.5cm) opening.

3. Roll the seam to the center back and press the tube flat.

4. Pin along the top and bottom.

5. Using a ½" (1.3cm) seam allowance, stitch along the top and bottom. Clip the corners and press the seam allowances flat (Figure 13).

6. Turn right-side out through that opening you left in the first seam. Gently poke out the corners so they are nice and square. A long knitting needle or chopstick works well for this.

3" (7.5 cm)

Bow
Interfacing

Fold

Figure 12

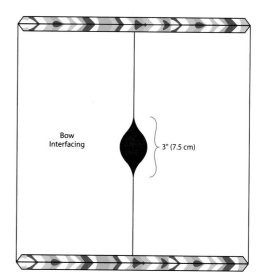

Bow
Interfacing

3" (7.5 cm)

Figure 13

7. Press flat, using a pressing cloth. Whipstitch the center opening closed (Figure 14).

8. Working from the back (the side with the seam), accordion fold the entire piece through the center. These folds are about 1" (2.5cm) each (Figure 15).

9. Wrap some thread around the center to hold the folds in place and set aside.

10. Find the 3½" × 3½" (9cm × 9cm) square for the faux knot. Fold right sides together and pin.

11. Using a ½" (1.3cm) seam allowance, stitch together to form a mini tube (Figure 16).

12. Turn right-side out. Find the accordion-folded bow. Wrap the strip around the center of the bow. Pin the raw edges together at the back of the bow.

13. Thread the hand-sewing needle and knot the end. Whipstitch the ends of the faux knot in place (Figure 17). The wrap will be, and should be, quite tight. Don't worry too much about the neatness of your stitches—they will be hidden.

Figure 14

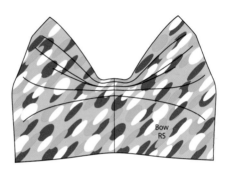

Figure 15

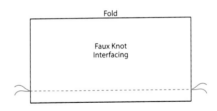

Figure 16

Figure 17

14. The bow will be positioned on the upper left-hand side of the pleated band, about 3" (7.5cm) from the left edge. The band itself will be gathered slightly at the point where the bow will sit.

15. If necessary, rethread the hand needle and knot the thread. At the 3" (7.5cm) in mark, run the needle and thread through all the pleats and pull taut to gather up the pleats (Figure 18).

16. Place the bow against the gathered point on the band, making sure the smooth front of the faux knot is facing out. Hand stitch the knot to the band.

17. Whipstitch along both the top and bottom inside edges of the knot (Figure 19). You are stitching just to the band.

18. When the bow is securely stitched to the band, reach inside the bag and tack the bow in place, stitching through the lining and batting into the back of the bow (Figure 20). You just need a few stitches, but it's important to anchor it through the layers of the bag in order to keep the large bow from flopping around.

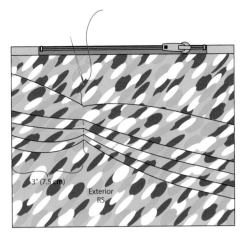

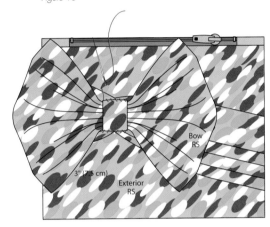

Figure 18

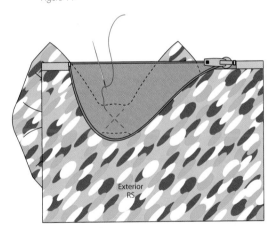

Figure 19

Figure 20

Boho Shoulder Bag

Want fun and casual? This bag's for you! Conquer expandable pockets using soft, fold-over elastic. Learn our stitch-flip-and-fuse method to create a super-flat front seam. The bag uses standard cotton—the brighter, the better—with the binding adding another pop of color. An adjustable D-ring strap lets you wear the bag on one shoulder or cross-body.

Finished Size
About 12" wide x 15" high x 2" deep (30.5cm x 38cm x 5cm)

Sewing Tools
General supplies listed on pages 8–10

Materials
¾ yard (68.5cm) cotton fabric for the large exterior panels front and back, the large exterior pocket and the front of the strap and tab

1 yard (91.5cm) cotton fabric for the small exterior panels front and back, the small exterior pocket, the back of the strap and tab, and the lining and lining pocket

2 D-rings, 1½" (3.8cm)

1 package fold-over elastic, 1" (2.5cm) wide

¾ yard (68.5cm) medium-weight fusible interfacing

All-purpose thread to match fabric and elastic

Project Notes

- We bought extra fabric (1¼ yards [1.1m] instead of ¾ yard [68.5cm]) in order to be able to cut our strap vertically to better capture the motif.

- Measurements are given as width x height.

Getting Started

1. From the fabric for the large exterior panels front and back, the large exterior pocket and the front of the strap and tab, cut the following:

   - 2 rectangles 8" × 16½" (20.5cm × 42cm) for the exterior panels
   - 1 rectangle 11" × 16" (28cm × 40.5cm) for the large exterior pocket
   - 1 strip 2" × WOF (width of fabric) (5cm × WOF) for the front of the strap
   - 1 strip 2" × 9" (5cm × 23cm) for the front of the strap tab

2. From the fabric for the small exterior panels front and back, the small exterior pocket, the back of the strap and tab, and the lining and lining pocket, cut the following:

   - 2 rectangles 6" × 16½" (15cm × 42cm) for the exterior panels
   - 1 rectangle 8" × 11" (20.5cm × 28cm) for the small exterior pocket
   - 2 rectangles 13" × 16½" (33cm × 42cm) for the lining
   - 1 rectangle 8" × 15" (20.5cm × 38cm) for the lining pocket
   - 1 strip 2" × WOF (5cm × WOF) for the back of the strap
   - 1 strip 2" × 9" (5cm × 23cm) for the back of the strap tab

3. From the interfacing, cut the following:

   - 2 rectangles 16" × 12" (40.5cm × 30.5cm)
   - 1 square 7" × 7" (18cm × 18cm)
   - 1 strip 1½" × 43" (3.8cm × 109cm)
   - 1 strip 1½" × 8" (3.8cm × 20.5cm)

4. From the fold-over elastic, cut the following:

   - 1 piece 8" (20.5cm)
   - 1 piece 6" (15cm)

   Leave the remaining length intact; you'll trim it later to exactly match the top of the bag.

Create the Lining

1. Find the 8" × 15" (20.5cm × 38cm) lining pocket and the 7" × 7" (18cm x 18cm) interfacing square. Fold the pocket in half, wrong sides together, so it is 8" × 7½" (20.5cm × 19cm), and press to set a crease.

2. Unfold wrong-side up so the crease line is visible. Center the interfacing square on the bottom half so one edge is aligning along the center crease with ½" (1.3cm) of fabric showing beyond the three remaining sides (Figure 1). Following the manufacturer's instructions, fuse in place.

3. Fold the interfaced pocket in half, right sides together, along the original crease line. Pin along both sides and across the bottom, leaving about a 3" (7.5cm) opening along the bottom for turning.

4. Using a ½" (1.3cm) seam allowance, stitch along both sides and across the bottom, pivoting at the corners. Your seam should run right along the edge of the interfacing. Remember to lock your seam on either side of the 3" (7.5cm) opening.

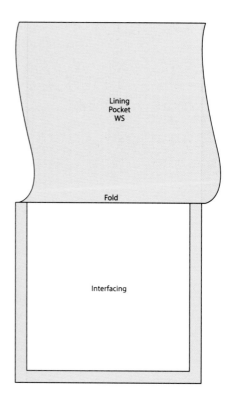

Figure 1

5. Clip the corners (Figure 2) and press open the seam allowance. Turn right-side out through the bottom opening. Push out the corners so they are nice and sharp. A chopstick or long knitting needle works well for this.

6. Fold in the raw edges of the opening so they are flush with the sewn seam. Press well.

7. Find the two 13" × 16½" (33cm × 42cm) lining panels. Place one panel right-side up and flat on your work surface. Measure to find the exact center of the panel.

8. Pin the pocket in place on the right side of the lining panel. Remember, the folded edge is the pocket top. Place the pocket centered side to side, with the bottom edge of the pocket 6" (15cm) up from the bottom raw edge of the fabric panel. Pin in place.

9. Edgestitch the pocket in place along both sides and across the bottom, pivoting at the corners and with a generous backstitch at the beginning and end of the seam, i.e., at the pocket top (Figure 3). This is a stress point for the pocket, and it's smart to secure the seam well. This edgestitching closes the opening used for turning.

10. Place the two lining pieces right sides together, sandwiching the pocket between the layers. Pin in place along both sides and across the bottom.

11. Using a ½" (1.3cm) seam allowance, stitch along both sides and across the bottom, pivoting at the corners (Figure 4). Press open the seam allowances.

12. Our bag is designed to have 2" (5cm) sides and base. To create this width, we figured our corners at 1" (2.5cm).

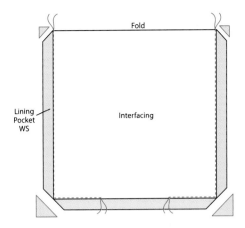

Figure 2

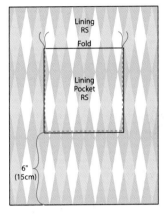

Figure 3

Figure 4

13. Using both hands, pinch and pull apart the bottom corner. As you pull, the fabric will begin to make a little peak with the corner point at the top and with the seam lines running down the middle. Center the side seam within this triangle peak. Make a mark 1" (2.5cm) from the peak.

14. Stitch along this line twice to reinforce and trim the excess (Figure 5).

15. Repeat Steps 13–14 to create the opposite boxed corner. Set the lining aside.

Add Elastic to the Front Pockets

1. Find the two exterior pocket pieces: the 11" × 16" (28cm × 40.5cm) large pocket and the 8" × 11" (20.5cm × 28cm) small pocket. Fold each in half, wrong sides together, so they are now 11" × 8" (28cm × 20.5cm) and 8" × 5½" (20.5cm × 14cm). Press well. The folded edge will be the bottom of each pocket.

2. Find the two cut pieces of fold-over elastic. The 8" (20.5cm) length is for the large pocket; the 6" (15cm) length is for the small pocket.

3. If necessary, rethread the machine with thread to best match the fold-over elastic in the top and bobbin.

4. There is a centerline woven into the design of most fold-over elastic. This line will help you fold the elastic exactly in half so you can use it as a binding for the top of the pocket. Fold the elastic in half and slip it over the raw edges of the large pocket. Align one cut end of the elastic with the side of the pocket (Figure 6). Pin the end in place.

5. Place this pinned end under the presser foot and drop the needle to help hold the layers in place. You can hold on to the pin as you start sewing to make sure your stitching grabs the elastic.

6. Grasp the free end of the elastic. Gently stretch the elastic so the fabric beneath it lays flat. Check again to make sure the elastic is correctly folded over the top raw edge of the pocket.

7. Begin stitching, stretching as you go. You may need to stop every so often, always with the needle in the down position so things don't shift, and restretch.

8. Stitch in this manner across the entire top of the pocket.

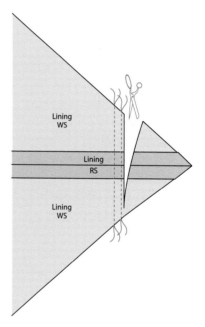

Figure 5

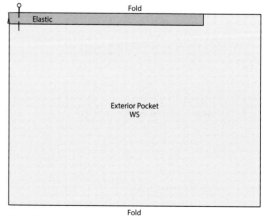

Figure 6

9. Trim the elastic flush with the fabric. When released, the pocket will be softly gathered across its top edge (Figure 7).

Note: Fold-over elastic is quite soft and easy to work with; it's even a little grippy. Over the short distance of our pockets, we didn't need to use any additional pins; we simply stretched and stitched, but feel free to add a few more for your own comfort level.

10. Repeat Steps 2–9 to bind the top of the smaller pocket.

11. Set both pockets aside.

Fuse the Exterior Panels

1. Find the two 8" × 16½" (20.5cm x 42cm) wide exterior panels and the two 12" × 16" (30.5cm × 40.5cm) interfacing panels. Place a fabric panel right-side down on your ironing board. Place an interfacing panel on the fabric (fusing side down). Align the top 8" (20.5cm) edge of the fabric with the interfacing, but shift the interfacing so there is ½" (1.3cm) of fabric showing along the bottom and the outer side (Figure 8). There will be a large portion of the interfacing extending beyond the fabric on the opposite side.

2. Following manufacturer's directions, fuse the interfacing to the fabric. Be careful with your iron so you are only fusing onto the fabric.

3. Flip the fabric panel over and press from the right side to make sure you have good adhesion.

4. Repeat Steps 1–3 with the remaining exterior panel and the remaining interfacing panel.

Attach the Front Pockets and Complete the Front and Back

1. Find the large bound pocket and the fused front panel. Place the panel right-side up.

2. Place the pocket on the panel so the sides of the pocket are flush with the sides of the fabric panel and the bottom of the pocket is 1¾" (4.5cm) up from the bottom raw edge of the fabric panel.

3. To take up the excess fabric at the bottom of the pocket, create about a 2½" (6.5cm) pleat at the bottom center of the pocket. To do this, simply find the center of the pocket, measure 1¼" (3.2cm) to the left and to the right of center and mark both points with a pin. Tuck under the pocket's excess fabric at both of these marked points until the bottom of the pocket lays flat against the fabric panel. Pin in place. Adjust the folds as needed to make sure your pleat is centered.

4. If necessary, rethread the machine with thread to best match the fabric in the top and bobbin.

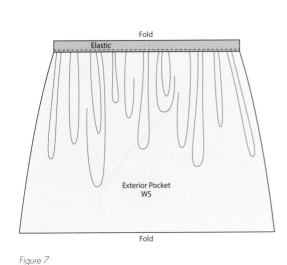

Figure 7

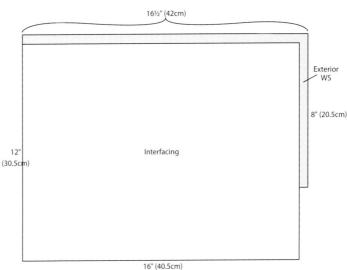

Figure 8

5. Edgestitch the pocket in place along both sides and across the bottom (Figure 9). Remember to pivot at the corners. The bottom stitching line will be visible, so be careful to keep your seam nice and straight. You may want to lengthen your stitch.

6. Find one of the 6" × 16½" (15cm × 42cm) exterior panels and the remaining pocket (the smaller pocket). Attach the pocket to the panel, following the same steps as above (Figure 10). The only difference is the pleat on this pocket will be only 2" (5cm) rather than 2½" (6.5cm).

7. Find both front sections with the pockets stitched in place.

8. Place the narrow panel over the wide panel, right sides together, sandwiching the pockets between the layers and aligning the inside raw edges. That extra interfacing is still extending to the right. Pin in place through all the layers.

9. Using a ½" (1.3cm) seam allowance, stitch the center seam through all the layers (including the interfacing) (Figure 11). Backstitch slightly when you stitch over the pocket tops, giving these stress points some extra strength.

10. Fold out the narrow panel over the interfacing and smooth flat. Iron to fuse the fabric to the interfacing (following the manufacturer's instructions) (Figure 12).

Note: Why did we choose this unusual fusing method? It allows our vertical seam to lay very flat without a bulky multi-layer seam allowance. This is a much better look when you have a seam that will be prominent on the face of a bag.

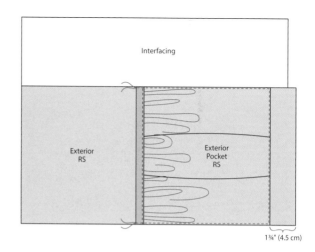

Figure 9

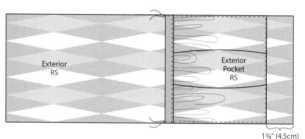

Figure 10

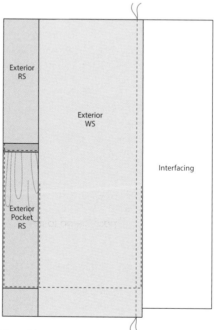

Figure 11

11. Find the remaining exterior panel and the remaining narrow panel (the ones without pockets). Following the same steps, stitch the center seam (Figure 13).

12. Then fold out and press to fuse.

Make and Place the Strap and Strap Tab

1. Find both the strap and strap-tab fabric strips and the corresponding interfacing strips. Place both sets of the fabric strips right sides together. Pin along one long side.

Note: We show the smaller strap tab in the illustrations. The steps are the same for the initial construction of both the strap and the strap tab.

2. Using a ¼" (6mm) seam allowance, stitch along the one long side.

3. Press open, pressing the seam allowance together and to one side.

4. Slip the interfacing up against the seam, centering it side to side and making sure an even ¼" (6mm) of fabric is showing along the long raw edge. Following the manufacturer's instructions, fuse the interfacing in place.

5. Press back both of the long raw edges ¼" (6mm).

6. Press back both short ends (all the way across both pieces) (Figure 14).

7. Fold the strap wrong sides together again along the seam line, aligning the folded edges on all sides. The folded edges should be perfectly flush. If they are not lining up, adjust one or both edges until they match.

8. You should now have a 1½" (3.8cm) strap tab with finished folded edges on all sides. Press well.

9. Edgestitch around all four sides, pivoting at the corners (Figure 15). (Remember, you are making both the strap tab and the strap.)

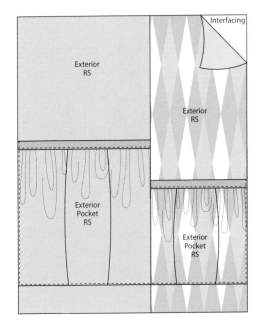

Figure 12

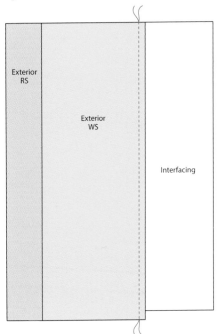

Figure 13

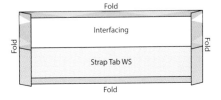

Figure 14

Figure 15

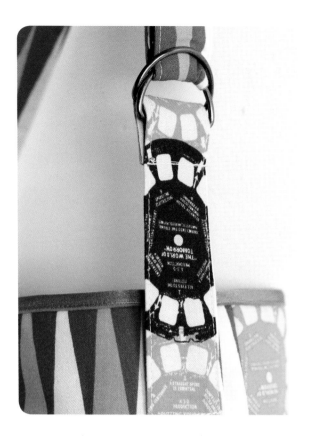

10. Find the two D-rings. Slip one end of the strap tab through both rings and fold it back on itself 1" (2.5cm). Stitch across to secure (Figure 16).

Note: Remember, in our design, the front of the strap is the fabric that matches the wide exterior panel. The back of the strap is the fabric that matches the narrow exterior panel and the lining. Keep track of this so you fold back the strap tab with the correct side facing out.

11. Find the two finished exterior panels. On the front panel (the panel with the pockets), pin the strap tab within the narrow panel. Place it 1" (2.5cm) in from the side raw edge with the bottom end of the strap tab 4" (10cm) down from the top raw edge of the fabric panel. Stitch the end in place with a 2" (5cm) X box (Figure 17).

12. Place one end of the long strap on the back panel in exactly the same position: within the narrow panel, 1" (2.5cm) in from the side, and 4" (10cm) down from the top. Stitch the end in place with a 2" (5cm) X box (Figure 18).

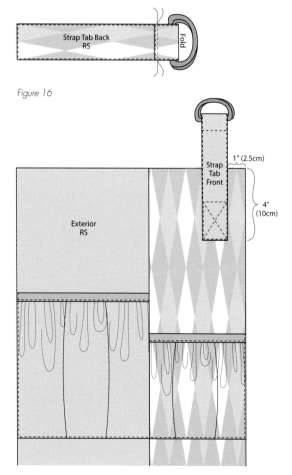

Figure 16

Figure 17

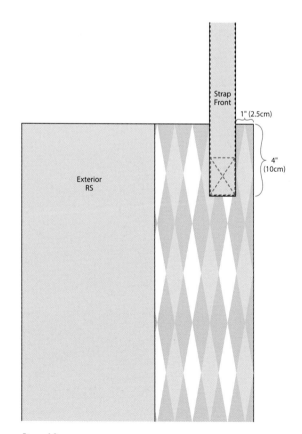

Figure 18

Assemble the Bag

1. Place the front and back exterior panels right sides together, aligning the sides and bottom. Pin in place. Pull the straps up through the top opening to keep them out of the way of the seam.

2. Using a ½" (1.3cm) seam allowance, stitch along both sides and across the bottom, pivoting at the corners. (Figure 19).

3. Following the same steps as above for the lining, create 2" (5cm) box corners.

4. With the exterior bag right-side out and the lining wrong-side out, slip the lining inside the exterior so the two bags are now wrong sides together.

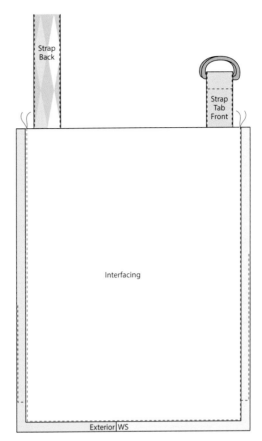

Figure 19

5. Align all the seams and the bottom corners. Make sure the strap and strap tab are folded out of the way of the top seam. Pin around the entire top of the bag (Figure 20).

6. Find the remaining length of fold-over elastic. You will use this to bind the top, similar to how you did for the pockets but without the stretch. We found it was a bit easier to stitch the elastic in place working with the bag inside out. So with the top still pinned, turn the whole shootin' match wrong-side out.

7. Starting at the point right above where the long strap is stitched in place, wrap the elastic over the raw edges of the bag/lining. Just as you did with the pocket, use the centerline that is woven into the elastic as your center guideline.

8. Wrap and pin around the entire top of the bag. When you come back around to your starting point (behind the strap), leave the tail long. As with the pockets, if you are a more experienced sewer, you may find you don't really need a lot of pins. The elastic is soft and grippy; it's easy to simply wrap as you go.

9. Stitch all the way around the top, keeping your seam close to the bottom edge of the elastic binding. Go slowly and carefully, making sure you are catching both the front and back of the binding. Stop and lock your seam just before you stitch over your starting point.

10. Remove the bag from the machine and carefully trim back the excess elastic so the two ends butt together.

11. Make one final tiny zigzag seam vertically across where the ends butt together to secure and prevent any raveling. If you started in the right place as described above, this seam will be hidden behind the strap. Turn the bag right-side out (Figure 21).

12. Slip the free end of the long strap through the top of the D-rings and adjust for your best fit.

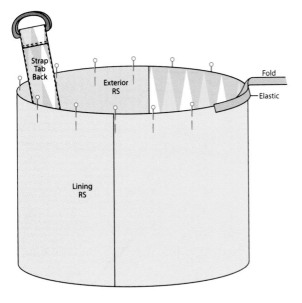

Figure 20

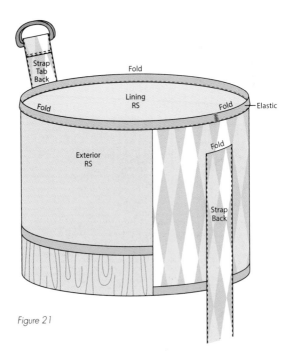

Figure 21

Jumbo Shopper with Inset Zipper

For everyday errands or weekend excursions, this multitasking tote is large and in charge and up to any job. Heavier-weight fabrics—we used canvas and faux leather—provide style and stability. The long loop handles are secured in a seam so they can hold lots. And you will learn how to put in an inset zipper, one of the hallmarks of a professional bag.

Finished Size

About 15" high × 18" wide × 5" deep (38cm × 45.5cm × 12.5cm) at the base; 23" (58.5cm) wide at the top; 20" (51cm) handle loops

Sewing Tools

Clips for use with the faux leather

Zipper foot

Edge-guide foot, optional

Quarter-inch seam foot, optional

Walking or even-feed foot, optional

General supplies listed on pages 8–10

Materials

1 yard (91.5cm) medium-weight canvas or similar, 54"+ (137cm+) wide, for the exterior top and zipper inset

½ yard (45.5cm) light- to medium-weight faux leather or similar, 54"+ (137cm+) wide, for the bag exterior base

1½ yards (1.4m) quilting-weight cotton for the lining

1 yard (91.5cm) low-loft batting

¼ yard (23cm) medium-weight linen or similar for the straps

⅓ yard (30.5cm) medium-weight fusible interfacing for the straps and lining pockets

1 separating sport zipper, 24" (61cm)

¼ yard (23cm) ⅛" (3mm) ribbon for the zipper pull, optional

All-purpose thread to match fabric

All-purpose thread to contrast with fabric for topstitching

Project Notes

- The yardage for the exterior allows for fussy cutting.

- We straight cut our two strap lengths. If you choose a heavier fabric that doesn't need interfacing and is less flexible, get 1 yard (91.5cm) in order to bias cut the straps.

- Rather than make your own straps, you could use 2½ yards (2.3m) of a 1½" (3.8cm) heavy twill tape or soft cotton webbing.

- We used a natural color thread for all topstitching on the canvas and straps and a taupe color for topstitching on the faux leather.

- Measurements are given as width × height.

Getting Started

1. From the fabric for the exterior top and zipper inset, fussy cut the following:

   - 2 rectangles 25" x 10" (63.5cm x 25.5cm) for the main tote panels
   - 2 strips 25" x 2" (63.5cm x 5cm) for the top facing
   - 4 strips 25" x 1½" (63.5cm x 3.8cm) for the zipper trim strips

   Note: We carefully cut our zipper trim strips to center the dots across the zipper.

2. From the fabric for the exterior base, cut the following:

   - 2 rectangles 25" x 9½" (63.5cm x 24cm) for the main exterior base panels
   - 2 rectangles 4" x 2½" (10cm x 6.5cm) for the zipper tabs

3. From the fabric for the lining, cut the following:

   - 2 rectangles 25" x 17½" (63.5cm x 44.5cm) for the lining
   - 1 rectangle 8" x 13" (20.5cm x 33cm) for the lining pocket

4. From the fabric for the straps, cut 2 strips 3½" x 43" (9cm x 109cm).

5. From the batting, cut the following:

   - 2 rectangles 24" x 17½" (61cm x 44.5cm) for the main panels
   - 2 squares 1½" x 1½" (3.8cm x 3.8cm) for the zipper tabs

6. From the interfacing, cut the following:

   - 2 strips 1¼" x 43" (3.2cm x 109cm) for the straps
   - 1 rectangle 7" x 6" (18cm x 15cm) for the lining pocket

Create the Inset Zipper Unit

1. Find the zipper and the four 25"x 1½" (63.5cm x 3.8cm) zipper trim strips. On each zipper trim strip, fold back each end ½" (1.3cm) and press in place.

2. Place one trim strip right-side up on your work surface. Center the zipper right-side up on top of the trim strip.

Make sure the folded ends of the fabric strip completely clear the zipper stops both top and bottom. The raw edge of the strip should be flush with the edge of the top zipper tape.

3. Find a second trim strip. Place this trim strip wrong-side up against the zipper.

4. You have sandwiched the top side of the zipper between the two strips. The two trim strips should be right sides together and with their folded ends flush with one another. Pin in place through all the layers.

5. Stitch through all the layers along the one side. Start with the zipper about halfway open. Stitch to the middle, where you're approaching the zipper pull. Stop with your needle in the down position. Lift up your presser foot. Twist your fabric around slightly in order to be able to carefully close the zipper. Reposition your fabric and finish sewing to the end (Figure 1).

Note: We used our regular presser foot and shifted our needle position as close to the zipper teeth as possible. You could also use a zipper foot, but with the chunkier sport-type zipper, we wanted to be a bit farther away from the teeth (about ¼" [6mm] from the teeth) than with a standard zipper. We found using the edge of our regular presser foot, with the needle position set to the far left, was a good guide to run along the edge of the zipper teeth.

6. Fold the two trim pieces away from the zipper teeth so these two pieces are now wrong sides together. The long raw edges should be flush as should the folded ends. Press flat.

Note: Throughout the project, be careful not to touch the hot iron directly to the zipper teeth. The plastic can melt, fusing the zipper permanently closed!

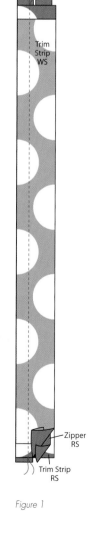

Figure 1

7. Repeat to attach the remaining two zipper trim strips to the opposite side of the zipper, taking care to make sure the ends of this second set of trim strips are exactly aligned with the first set (Figure 2).

8. Rethread with contrasting thread for topstitching; we used a natural to match the dots of our motif.

9. With both zipper trim pieces pressed away from the zipper teeth, edgestitch across the folded ends, then pivot and edgestitch along the zipper seam (Figure 3). Our careful fussy cutting of the zipper trim strips creates a match across the zipper.

10. Find the two 4" × 2½" (10cm × 6.5cm) zipper tabs and the 1½" × 1½" (3.8cm × 3.8cm) batting squares. Place a batting square on the wrong side of each zipper tab. It should be ½" (1.3cm) from one short end and centered side to side.

Note: The batting is grippy enough to stay in place against the wrong side of the faux leather for the tab construction steps. However, you could use a small piece of seam tape to hold it more securely.

11. Place one tab wrong-side up against the wrong side of the zipper at one end (Figure 4).

12. Flip the zipper right-side up. The tab should be centered within the zipper strip, and the end of the tab should be flush with the extending end of the zipper tape. Pin or clip in place.

13. Sew the tab to the end of the zipper, working from the right side of the zipper. Run the seam right along the folded and edgestitched ends of the zipper trim strips, which should be just above the zipper stop. You are only stitching across the width of the zipper itself (Figure 5).

Note: You are stitching over the zipper. The teeth are plastic and will allow the needle to stitch; however, go slowly and carefully. If necessary, you can even hand walk the needle, using the handwheel on the machine.

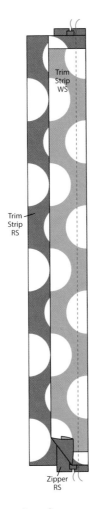

Figure 2

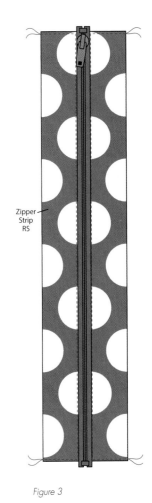

Figure 3

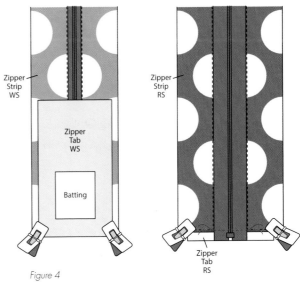

Figure 4

Figure 5

14. Fold up the tab along the seam, then fold in the sides of the tab so they are aligned with the width of the zipper. Pin or clip in place (Figure 6).

15. Fold down the top raw edge of the tab about ½" (1.3cm) to create a final finished edge, then fold the tab in half. The folded-down edge of the tab should sit just beyond the folded and edgestitched ends of the zipper trim strips, as shown. Adjust the fold of the tab as necessary to create this placement. The folded side edges of the tab should also be flush. Pin or clip in place.

16. If necessary, rethread the machine with thread to best match the tab in the top and bobbin.

17. Edgestitch around all four sides of the tab to secure (Figure 7). Go slowly and carefully. There are a lot of layers, and you are stitching right along an edge. As above, you can even hand walk the needle across the zipper teeth.

18. Repeat Steps 10–17 to attach the remaining tab to the opposite end of the zipper, trimming away the excess zipper tape as necessary.

Make and Attach the Straps

1. Find the two 3½" × 43" (9cm × 109cm) fabric strips and the 1¼" × 43" (3.2cm × 109cm) interfacing strips. Fold one fabric strip in half lengthwise, wrong sides together, to set a center crease. Open wrong-side up so the crease line is visible.

2. Insert an interfacing strip. The ends of the interfacing should be flush with the ends of the fabric, and one long edge should align with the center crease. There will be ½" (1.3cm) of fabric showing beyond the interfacing on the opposite long edge. Following the manufacturer's instructions, fuse the interfacing strips in place.

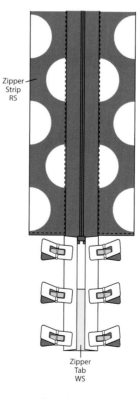

Zipper Strip RS

Zipper Tab WS

Figure 6

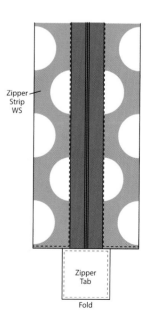

Zipper Strip WS

Zipper Tab

Fold

Figure 7

3. Fold back each long raw edge ½" (1.3cm) and press well (Figure 8). The ends remain raw and unfolded.

4. Refold along the original center crease line. The folded edges should be flush.

5. If necessary, rethread the machine with thread to best match the straps in the top and bobbin.

6. Create four parallel lines of topstitching the length of each strap.

Note: We lengthened our stitch to 3.0mm, and opted to use an edge-guide foot to keep our measurements precise. As an option, you could use a fabric pen or pencil to draw in guidelines and use a standard presser foot. When drawing, remember that you are working on the right side of the fabric; make sure you choose a marker that will easily wipe away or vanish with exposure to the air.

7. Start by stitching a line ⅛" (3mm) in from each outside edge.

8. Then stitch a second pair of lines, each ⅜" (1cm) in from each outside edge (don't measure from the previous stitching lines—measure from the outside edge of the strap) (Figure 9).

9. Repeat Steps 1–8 to create a second strap with four identical lines of topstitching.

10. Find the upper exterior panels. Find the panel's center point. Then measure 2½" (6.5cm) to the right of center and 2½" (6.5cm) to the left of center. At these right and left points, use a fabric pen or pencil to draw a vertical line from the top of the panel to the bottom.

11. Align the inside edge of a strap along these drawn lines. The bottom raw edges of the strap should be flush with the bottom raw edge of the fabric panel. Make sure there are no twists in the strap's loop.

12. Measure 1½" (3.8cm) down from the top raw edge of the panel along each side of the strap. At this point, place a horizontal pin or draw in a guide line. This marks the stopping point for the topstitching that will attach the strap.

13. The machine should still be threaded with the same thread used for the strap's four lines of topstitching.

14. Edgestitch each side of the strap in place, following exactly along the strap's topstitching. Start at the bottom, go up one side, pivot and cross at the horizontal marking point, pivot at the opposite topstitching guideline and continue down to the bottom (Figure 10).

15. Repeat steps 10–14 to attach the remaining strap to the other top exterior panel.

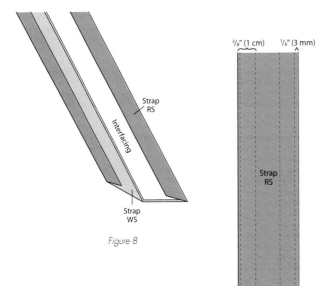

Figure 8

Figure 9

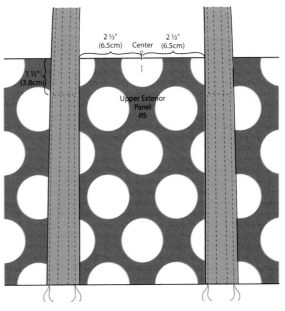

Figure 10

Complete the Exterior Panels

1. Find the two faux leather bottom panels and the two canvas upper panels. Place one faux leather panel right sides together with one canvas panel, aligning them along one 25" (63.5cm) edge and sandwiching the straps out of the way between the layers. Pin or clip in place (Figure 11).

Note: If you are using a directional print, you would align the bottom of the top canvas panel to the top of the faux leather panel.

2. Switch to a walking foot or similar. For best results, sew with the faux leather down against the feed dogs and the canvas side up under the needle.

3. Using a ½" (1.3cm) seam allowance, stitch together each pair of panels. Finger press the seam down toward the faux leather.

4. Rethread the machine with contrasting thread in the top and bobbin for the faux leather (we used a taupe). Topstitch ¼" (6mm) away from the seam within the faux leather (Figure 12).

5. Place each sewn exterior panel right-side down and flat on your work surface. Center one rectangle of batting over each panel and lightly press flat. There should be ½" (1.3cm) of fabric showing beyond the batting on all four sides.

6. Pin or clip the batting in place.

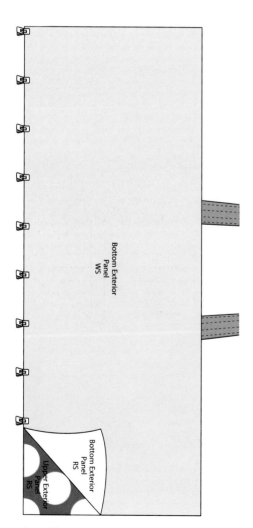

Figure 11

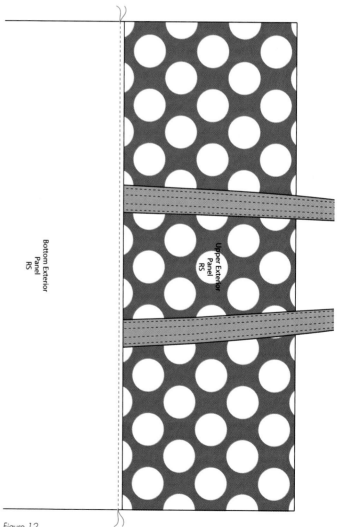

Figure 12

Seam and Box the Corners of the Exterior Bag

1. Place the front and back exterior panels right sides together. Be very careful to line up the horizontal seams. Re-pin or clip in place, keeping the batting layers in the same position with ½" (1.3cm) of fabric showing all the way around. Pull the straps up and out of the way.

2. Using a ½" (1.3cm) seam allowance, stitch both sides and across the bottom, pivoting at the corners (Figure 13).

3. With the sewn fabric still right sides together, using both hands, pinch and pull apart the corner. As you pull, the fabric will begin to make a little peak with the corner point at the top and the seam lines running down the middle of the front and the back. Match

these side and bottom seams. Place a pin in the seams to hold them together. It is very important that you exactly match the seams; that is what will make the lines of your finished corner look good. Our bag is designed to have 5" (12.5cm) sides and base. To create this width, we figured our corners at 2½" (6.5cm). Measure this distance from the triangle peak and mark. Stitch along the drawn line twice and trim away the excess (Figure 14).

4. Repeat Step 3 to create the opposite corner.

5. Fold back the upper edge wrong sides together ½" (1.3cm) all the way around and press well.

6. Turn the bag right-side out and push the corners out into place.

7. Set the exterior bag aside.

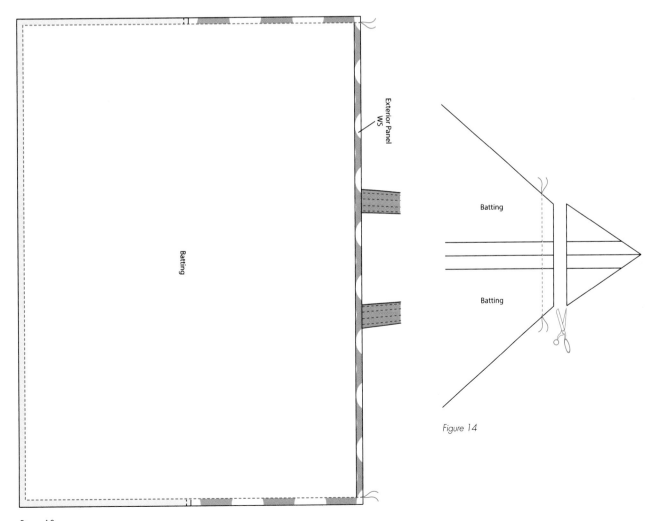

Exterior Panel WS

Batting

Batting

Batting

Figure 13

Figure 14

Assemble the Lining and Upper Facing

1. Find the 8" × 13" (20.5cm × 33cm) pocket rectangle and the 7" × 6" (18cm × 15cm) interfacing rectangle. Fold the fabric panel in half, wrong sides together, so it is now 8" × 6½" (20.5cm × 16.5cm). Press to set a center crease. Open up the fabric wrong-side up so the crease is visible.

2. Place the interfacing rectangle against one half, aligning one 7" (18cm) side with the center crease. There should be ½" (1.3cm) of fabric extending beyond the interfacing on the other three sides. Following the manufacturer's instructions, fuse in place.

3. Refold right sides together. Pin along all three sides, leaving a 3" (7.5cm) opening along the bottom for turning.

4. Using a ½" (1.3cm) seam allowance, stitch along both sides and across the bottom, pivoting at the corners. Lock your seam on either side of the 3" (7.5cm) opening. Clip the corners (Figure 15).

5. Turn right-side out. Push out the corners so they are nice and sharp.

6. Fold in the raw edges of the opening so they are flush with the sewn seam. Press well.

7. Fold the pocket in half vertically and press lightly to set a vertical center crease line.

8. Find the two lining panels. Place one panel right-side up and flat on your work surface. Measure to find the exact center of the panel.

9. Place the pocket on the right side of one lining panel. The pocket should be centered side to side and 4" (10cm) down from the top raw edge. Pin in place.

10. Edgestitch the pocket in place along both sides and across the bottom, pivoting at the corners and with a generous backstitch at the beginning and end of the seam, i.e., at the pocket top. This is a stress point for the pocket, and it's smart to secure the seam well. This edgestitching closes the opening used for turning.

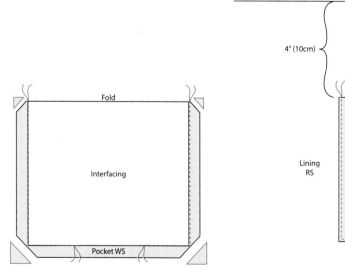

Figure 15

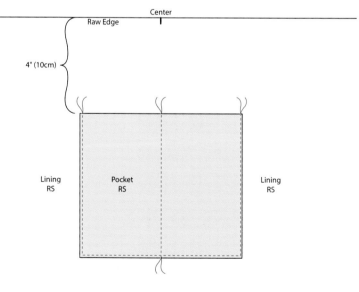

Figure 16

11. Stitch along the vertical crease line to divide the pocket into two sections (Figure 16).

12. Find the zipper unit. Place it right-side up on the right side of the lining/pocket panel. The zipper unit should be centered side to side on the lining panel with one side of the zipper unit flush with the top raw edge of the panel. Pin in place.

13. Find one of the two 25" × 2" (63.5cm × 5cm) facing strips. Place it right-side down over the zipper unit. The top raw edges of the lining, facing and zipper unit should be flush. Re-pin in place through all the layers.

14. Using a ½" (1.3cm) seam allowance, stitch across through all the layers (Figure 17).

15. Repeat steps 12–14 to attach the remaining raw edge of the zipper unit to the remaining lining panel, sandwiching the zipper unit as above with the remaining facing strip. When sewn and pressed away from the zipper unit, the two facing strips sit like little wings above the lining panels (Figure 18).

16. Fold the two lining pieces right sides together, sandwiching the pocket and zipper unit between the layers and matching the *ends* of the facing as well as the sides and bottom edges of the lining. Pin in place along both sides and across the bottom. Push the zipper tabs in and out of the way in order to pin all the way to the top of each side seam.

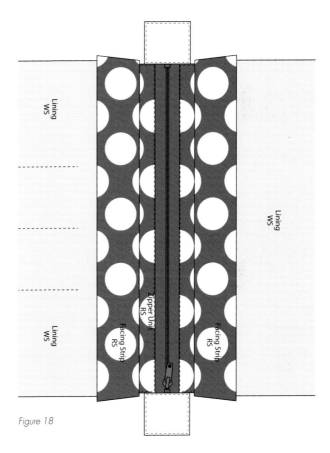

Figure 18

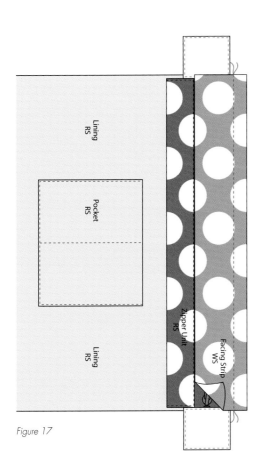

Figure 17

17. Using a ½" (1.3cm) seam allowance, stitch along both sides and across the bottom, pivoting at the corners (Figure 19).

Note: We recommend switching to a zipper foot with the needle in the left position to allow you to stitch on the seam line but avoid the bulk of the zipper tab.

18. Following the same steps as above for the exterior tote, measure for 5" (12.5cm) boxed corners. Create both boxed corners.

19. Fold down the top raw edge of the lining facing wrong sides together ½" (1.3cm) all the way around. Press in place (Figure 20).

20. With the lining still wrong-side out, find the exterior bag, which should be right-side out. Slip the lining inside the exterior bag so the two are now wrong sides together.

21. Smooth the lining all the way down into the exterior bag so the bottom boxed corners are aligned. Carefully align the top folded edges of both the exterior and the lining facing. If they are not perfectly flush, refold as necessary and re-press. Pin the layers together around the entire top opening (Figure 21).

22. If necessary, rethread with the same contrasting thread, used above to create the zipper unit, in the top and bobbin.

23. Open the zipper all the way. Topstitch around the entire top opening two times. The first time stitch about ⅛" (3mm) from the top folded edges. Go slowly, especially around the corners at the zipper tabs. The second time around, stitch about ⅛" (3mm) from the facing seam (Figure 22).

24. Make sure the handle/strap loops are folded out of the way of your stitching. We actually pinned our straps up to hold them in position and marked the existing horizontal strap seam with pins. The pins are just there as a guide and should be pulled out as you sew.

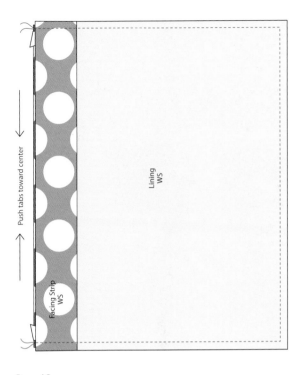

Push tabs toward center

Facing Strip
WS

Lining
WS

Figure 19

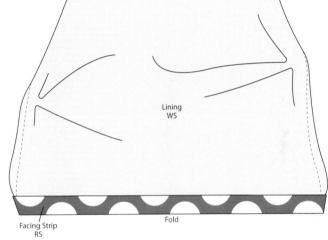

Lining
WS

Facing Strip
RS

Fold

Figure 20

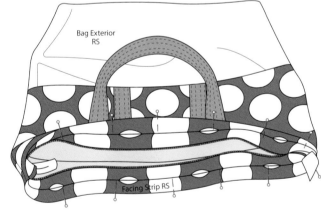

Bag Exterior
RS

Facing Strip RS

Figure 21

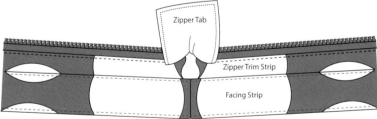

Zipper Tab

Zipper Trim Strip

Facing Strip

Figure 22

Urban-Style Messenger Bag

Slightly slouchy and majorly modern, our messenger bag has the fashion zen you need to carry a briefcase without it looking like a briefcase. Stay organized and stay cool. The project is full of light-bulb moments: make a classic adjustable strap, insert a magnetic snap, box bottom corners and create a full lining with a pocket. These are details every bag-maker loves.

Finished Size
About 14½" wide × 13" high × 2" deep (37cm × 33cm × 5cm)

Sewing Tools
Quarter-inch seam foot, optional

Zipper foot, optional for tight stitching next to the magnetic snap

General supplies listed on pages 8–10

Materials
1 ½ yards (1.4m) medium- to heavy-weight cotton twill, canvas, cotton duck or similar for the bag's exterior

1 yard (91.5cm) standard-weight cotton for the bag's lining and lining pockets

1 magnetic purse clasp

2 D-rings or rectangular rings, 1½" (3.8cm)

1 double-loop slider, 1½" (3.8cm)

2 decorative buttons, 1¼"–1½" (3.2cm–3.8cm)

2 yards (1.8m) medium-weight fusible interfacing, 20"+ (51cm+) wide

All-purpose thread to match fabrics

Project Notes

- A bold motif with proper fussy cutting is important to the design of the bag. Extra yardage is included in the given quantities to accommodate this. We used a linen/cotton canvas.

- We used D-rings rather than rectangular rings.

- Measurements are given as width × height.

Getting Started

1. From the fabric for the bag's exterior, fussy cut the following, carefully centering your fabric's main motif:

   - 2 rectangles 14" × 13" (35.5cm × 33cm) for the flap
   - 2 rectangles 18½" × 15½" (47cm × 39.5cm) for the main body panels
   - 1 rectangle 15" × 10" (38cm × 25.5cm) for the exterior pocket
   - 2 strips 6" × 3½" (15cm × 9cm) for the strap tabs
   - 1 strip 44" × 3½" (112cm × 9cm) for the strap (the width of the fabric in our sample)
   - 1 strip 17" × 3½" (43cm × 9cm) also for the strap

   Note: The two strap pieces will be pieced together to equal a final cut length of 60" (152.5cm). If your fabric is 60" (152.5cm) or greater, you can simply cut 1 strip 3½" × 60" (9cm × 152.5cm).

2. From the fabric for the bag's lining and lining pockets, cut the following:

   - 2 rectangles 18" × 15½" (45.5cm × 39.5cm)
   - 1 rectangle 15" × 17" (38cm × 43cm) for the larger lining pocket
   - 1 rectangle 11" × 15" (28cm × 38cm) for the smaller lining pocket

3. From the fusible interfacing, cut the following:

   - 2 strips 1½" × 5½" (3.8cm × 14cm) for the strap tabs
     1 strip 1½" × 44" (3.8cm × 112cm) for the strap
   - 1 strip 1½" × 17" (3.8cm × 43cm) also for the strap

   Note: You need interfacing for the length of the 60" (152.5cm) strap. Cut the interfacing to match the fabric lengths you cut above. We cut our fabric at 44" (112cm) and 17" (43cm) and so cut our interfacing to match.

   - 2 rectangles 18½" × 15½" (47cm × 39.5cm) for the main body panels
   - 1 rectangle 14" × 8½" (35.5cm × 21.5cm) for the exterior pocket
   - 1 rectangle 10" × 7½" (25.5cm × 19cm) for the smaller lining pocket
   - 1 rectangle 14" × 8" (35.5cm × 20.5cm) for the larger lining pocket
   - 1 rectangle 13" × 12" (33cm × 30.5cm) for the flap
   - 2 squares 2" × 2" (5cm × 5cm) to stabilize the magnetic snap

Create the Flap

1. Find the two 14" × 13" (35.5cm × 33cm) rectangles for the flap. Place them right sides together, making sure all the raw edges are flush.

2. Place the panels on your cutting mat in the proper orientation (14" [35.5cm] wide). Trim the bottom two corners at a 45-degree angle. You want to orient the cuts with your motif, centering the design and ensuring the two cuts are exact mirror images of one another. Our cuts were about 4" (10cm) along the diagonal.

   Note: Many cutting mats have 45-degree grid lines, which would be perfect to use for these cuts.

3. Using your see-through ruler and a rotary cutter, slice away the corners through both layers (Figure 1).

4. Repeat steps 1–3 to cut matching corners from the 13" × 12" (33cm × 30.5cm) interfacing rectangle.

   Note: It's easiest and most accurate to use a rotary cutter for these steps. If you do not have one, use a ruler to draw in cut lines to follow with your scissors.

5. Following the manufacturer's instructions, fuse the interfacing to the wrong side of one fabric flap panel. The interfacing should be centered on the fabric panel so there is ½" (1.3cm) of fabric showing beyond the edge of the interfacing on all sides.

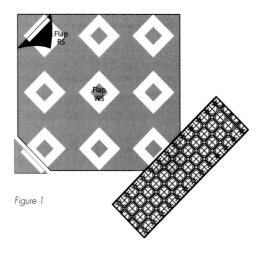

Figure 1

6. Place the two flap panels right sides together again, aligning all the raw edges. Pin in place along both sides and across the angled bottom.

7. Using a ½" (1.3cm) seam allowance, stitch both sides and across the angled bottom (Figure 2). Go slowly to maintain a consistent seam width, and remember to pivot at all the corners.

8. Trim the corners and press the seam allowance open.

9. Turn the flap right-side out through the top opening and press flat.

10. Using a ¼" (6mm) seam allowance, topstitch along the entire seam (along both sides and across the angled bottom, pivoting at all the corners) (Figure 3).

11. Set aside the finished flap.

Create and Place the Exterior Pocket

1. Find the 15" × 10" (38cm × 25.5cm) rectangle for the exterior pocket and the 14" × 8½" (35.5cm × 21.5cm) rectangle of interfacing.

2. Place the interfacing on the wrong side of the fabric panel, positioning the interfacing ½" (1.3cm) in from both sides and the bottom and 1" (2.5cm) down from the top. Following the manufacturer's instructions, fuse the interfacing in place.

Note: This exterior pocket is not lined, so you may want to finish the raw edges of the pocket panel. We used a simple zigzag stitch.

3. Fold back the edges of the fabric panel along the edge of the interfacing. In other words, fold back the sides and bottom ½" (1.3cm) and fold back the top 1" (2.5cm) along the edge of the interfacing. Press the folds (Figure 4).

4. When all the sides are pressed, flip over the pocket and topstitch the top 1" (2.5cm) hem in place.

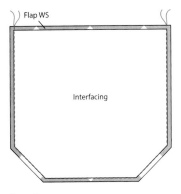

Figure 2

Figure 3

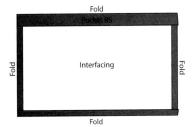

Figure 4

5. Find the two 18½" × 15½" (47cm × 39.5cm) main body panels and the two 18½" × 15½" (47cm × 39.5cm) rectangles of interfacing. Following the manufacturer's instructions, fuse the interfacing to the wrong side of each body panel. The interfacing should be flush with the fabric all the way around.

6. Place one of the main body panels right-side up on your work surface. Place the exterior pocket right-side up on the body panel. Position the pocket so it sits 2¼" (5.5cm) up from the bottom raw edge of the body panel and is centered side to side (2¼" [5.5cm] in from each side). Pin the pocket in place.

7. Find the exact center of the pocket and draw a vertical line through the pocket at this point. Use your see-through ruler and a fabric pen or pencil. You are working on the right side of the fabric, so be sure the writing tool will easily wipe or wash away or vanish with exposure to the air.

8. Edgestitch the pocket in place along both sides and across the bottom. Remember to pivot at the corners. It's also a good idea to use a generous backstitch at the start and end (the top corners of the pocket), as these are pocket stress points.

9. Topstitch along the drawn centerline, dividing the pocket into two sections. For the cleanest look, use a lock stitch at the beginning and end, or leave your thread tails long and knot to secure (Figure 5).

Assemble the Main Panels and Box the Corners

1. Place the two exterior panels right sides together. Pin along both sides and across the bottom.

2. Using a ½" (1.3cm) seam allowance, stitch both sides and across the bottom, pivoting at the corners (Figure 6).

3. Create 3" (7.5cm) box corners, which means your "box" will be half that size or 1½" (3.8cm).

   With the sewn fabric still right sides together, using both hands, pinch and pull apart the corner. As you pull, the fabric will begin to make a little peak with the corner point at the top and the seam lines running down the middle of the front and the back. Match

Figure 5

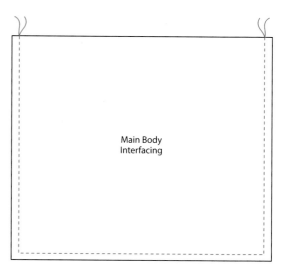

Figure 6

these side and bottom seams. Place a pin in the seams to hold them together. It is very important that you exactly match the seams; that is what will make the lines of your finished corner look good. Measure and mark a line 1½" (3.8cm) from the triangle peak. Stitch this line twice for reinforcement. Trim away the excess close to the second seam (Figure 7).

4. Turn the main bag right-side out, push out the corners and press.

Make Straps and Strap Tabs

1. For the strap tabs, find the two 6" × 3½" (15cm × 9cm) fabric strips and the two 5½" × 1½" (14cm × 3.8cm) strips of interfacing.

2. Place a fabric strip wrong-side up on your work surface. Place the interfacing on the upper half of the strip so it sits ¼" (6mm) down from the top raw edge and ¼" (6mm) in from each raw side edge. Following the manufacturer's instructions, fuse the interfacing in place.

3. Fold the fabric strip in half, right sides together. Pin in place along the side and one end.

4. Using a ¼" (6mm) seam allowance, stitch across the end and down the side, pivoting at the corner (Figure 8).

5. Repeat steps 2–4 to create the second tab.

6. Clip the corners and press open the seam allowances (Figure 9).

7. Turn the tabs right side out through the open ends. Use a long, blunt tool, such as a chopstick or knitting needle, to gently push out the corners. Press both tabs flat.

8. Edgestitch along both sides and both ends (including the raw end) (Figure 10). We used a contrasting thread and lengthened our stitch.

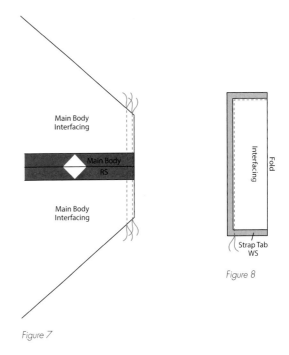

Figure 7

Figure 8

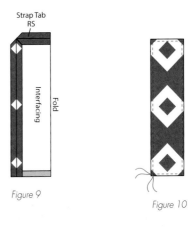

Figure 9

Figure 10

9. For the long strap, as mentioned above, unless your fabric was wide enough to cut one 60" (152.5cm) strip, you will need to piece two lengths of fabric to create the finished 60" (152.5cm). We used a 3½" × 44" (9cm × 112cm) length and a 3½" × 17" (9cm × 43cm) length.

10. Find the fabric strips as well as the corresponding 1½" (3.8cm) interfacing strips. Following the manufacturer's instructions, fuse the interfacing to the wrong side of the fabric strips. The inside edge of the interfacing should sit at the center of the fabric strip; the outside edge of the interfacing should sit ¼" (6mm) in from the outside raw edge of the fabric.

Note: Folding the fabric strips in half lengthwise and lightly pressing to set a center crease can help with perfect placement.

11. Attach the two strips as you would two lengths of binding. The two lengths should be at right angles to one another, right sides together. Pin in place, then stitch across from top to bottom on the diagonal.

12. Trim back the seam allowance to ¼" (6mm) (Figure 11), open out and press flat.

13. Fold the strap right sides together and stitch down the long side; leave both ends open and raw. Turn right-side out through an open end. Press the long strap flat.

14. Edgestitch along both sides and across both ends. As above with the strap tabs, we used a contrasting thread and lengthened our stitch.

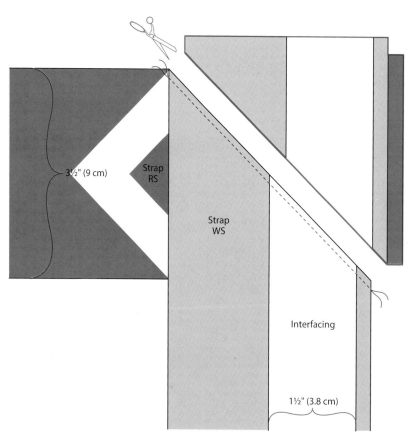

Figure 11

15. Find the slider and the two D-rings. Turn under one raw end of the strap 1½" (3.8cm). Loop this folded end through the center of the slider and pin in place against the back of the strap.

16. Stitch across the folded end to secure the slider in place. Use two lines of stitching and work on the right side of the strap. One line of stitching should be close to the folded edge; the second should be ¼"–½" (6mm–1.3cm) from the first seam (Figure 12).

17. With the strap laying wrong-side up (so you can see the folded-under end), find one of the D-rings. Thread the opposite raw end, bottom up, through the D-ring (Figure 13).

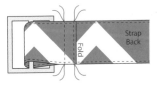

Figure 12

Figure 13

18. Pull the strap through so it is now facing right-side up and feed the end back through the slider, going up and over the folded end (Figure 14). This creates your adjusting loop.

19. Find the remaining D-ring. Feed the raw end of the strap through the curved end of this D-ring, and edgestitch in place, just as you did to secure the slider. Before stitching, check to make sure there are no twists in your strap (Figure 15).

20. Find the two strap tabs. Thread one tab through the flat side of each D-ring. Fold the tab together. The raw tab edge should sit about ¼" (6mm) from the finished tab edge (Figure 16). This will allow the raw edge to be concealed when the tab is sewn on the bag.

21. Find the exterior bag. Place a tab at each side seam. The tab should be centered over the seam, and the finished end of the tab should sit 2" (5cm) down from the top raw edge of the bag. Pin the tab in place.

22. Secure each tab in place with about a 1¼" × ¾" (3.2cm × 2cm) *X* box of stitching (Figure 17).

23. Thread a hand-sewing needle and stitch a decorative button at the center of the *X* box through all the layers.

Figure 14

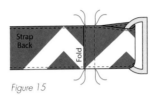

Figure 15

Figure 16

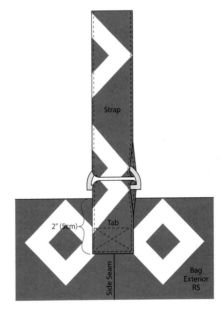

Figure 17

Create the Lining

1. Find the two lining pockets and their corresponding interfacing rectangles. Center the interfacing on the wrong side of each fabric panel. Place the interfacing on the top half of the fabric panel ½" (1.3cm) down from the top raw edge and ½" (1.3cm) in from each side. Following the manufacturer's instructions, fuse in place.

2. Each pocket is constructed in the same manner. Fold each pocket in half, right sides together, matching all the raw edges. Pin in place along both sides and across the bottom.

3. Rethread with thread to best match the lining in the top and bobbin. Reset the stitch length to normal. Using a ½" (1.3cm) seam allowance, sew both sides and across the bottom, leaving a 3" (7.5cm) opening along the bottom for turning. Clip the corners (Figure 18).

4. Turn each pocket right-side out through the bottom opening. Push out the corners so they are nice and sharp. A chopstick or long knitting needle works well for this. Fold in the raw edges of the pocket openings so they are flush with the sewn seam. Press both pockets flat.

5. Find the two lining panels. Position the smaller pocket on one lining panel, placing it 4½" (11.5cm) down from the top raw edge of its lining panel and 4" (10cm) in from each side.

6. Pin the smaller pocket in place along both sides and across the bottom.

7. Using the see-through ruler and a marking pen or pencil, find the exact center of the pocket and draw a vertical line to divide the pocket into two sections.

8. Stitch along the drawn dividing line, then edgestitch the pocket in place along both sides and across the bottom, pivoting at the corners (Figure 19). This closes the pocket opening used for turning right-side out.

9. Position the larger pocket on the remaining lining panel, placing it 2¼" (5.5cm) up from the bottom raw edge of the lining panel and 2¼" (5.5cm) in from each side.

10. Using the see-through ruler and a marking pen or pencil, measure 9" (23cm) in from the left side and draw a vertical line to divide the pocket into two sections: one large and one small.

11. As above, stitch along the drawn dividing line. Edgestitch the pocket in place along both sides and across the bottom, pivoting at the corners (Figure 20).

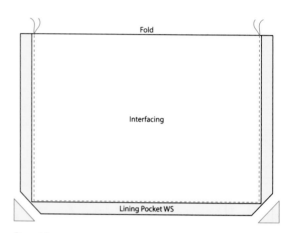

Figure 18

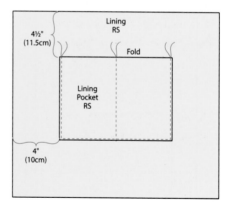

Figure 19

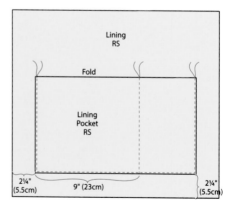

Figure 20

13. Place the two lining panels right sides together, sandwiching the pockets between the layers. Pin along both sides and across the bottom.

14. Using a ½" (1.3cm) seam allowance, stitch both sides and across the bottom, pivoting at the corners (Figure 21).

15. As you did for the exterior bag, create 3" (7.5cm) box corners, which means your box will be half that size or 1½" (3.8cm) .

16. Turn the lining right-side out, push out the corners and press.

17. Fold down the top raw edge of the lining wrong sides together ½" (1.3cm) all the way around.

18. Measure to find the exact center of both the front and back of the lining. Place a pin at each point.

19. Find the two 2" (5cm) squares of interfacing. Fuse one square to the wrong side of the lining at each of the center points. The interfacing should be tucked up under the fold.

20. Find the magnetic purse snap. Following the manufacturer's instructions, insert one half at each center point of the lining. The top curve of the snap back should be ⅝" (1.5cm) down from the top folded edge of the lining (Figure 22).

21. Insert the snap halves from the front through to the back following the manufacturer's instructions (Figure 23).

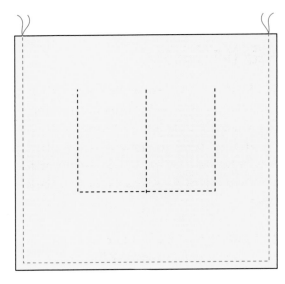

Figure 21

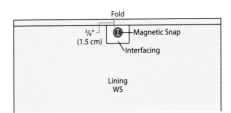

Figure 22

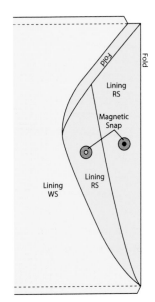

Figure 23

Attach the Flap and Finish

1. Find the exterior bag; it should be right-side out. Fold down the top raw edge of the exterior bag wrong sides together ½" (1.3cm) all the way around.

2. Find the flap. Measure to find the exact center along the flap's straight raw edge. Mark this point with a pin.

3. Place the raw edge of the flap flush with the folded-down top edge of the exterior bag. Pin the flap in place against the back exterior panel.

4. Baste the flap in place (Figure 24).

5. Find the lining, and turn it wrong-side out. Slip the lining inside the exterior so the two bags are now wrong sides together. Align the side seams and the bottom boxed corners. The magnetic snap halves should be at the center front and back, and the two lining pockets should be facing one another.

6. Bring the lining up into place over the flap and pin the lining to the exterior all the way around the top of the bag (Figure 25). The folded edges of the two layers should be perfectly flush. If they don't line up, simply roll one or both folds until they align.

7. Topstitch around the entire top opening of the bag through all the layers, staying as close to the folded edges as possible (Figure 26). We were able to use our standard presser foot, but if you feel you might have trouble stitching past the magnetic snap, switch to a zipper foot. As with the strap tabs, we used a contrasting thread and lengthened our stitch.

Figure 24

Figure 25

Figure 26

Trendy Cinch-Top Bucket Bag

Straight off the shelves of the highest of high-end boutiques, this dramatic bucket bag shows how you can translate current trends with your DIY skills. Our chic faux leather vinyl sews with ease thanks to a few tricks of the trade, including glue and markers! Metal grommets form the unique cinched top, and snaps adjust the strap. Friends won't believe it's handmade.

Finished Size

About 10" wide × 12" high × 6" deep (25.5cm × 30.5cm × 15cm) with 46" (117cm) strap

Sewing Tools

Walking or even-feed foot, optional

Nonstick presser foot, optional

General supplies listed on pages 8–10

Materials

¾ yard (68.5cm) medium-weight flexible vinyl or similar, 54"+ (137cm+) wide, for the bag exterior and strap

½ yard (45.5cm) standard-weight cotton for the lining

4 D-rings, 1" (2.5cm)

5 heavy-duty, smooth-cap snaps

12 large metal eyelets

4 purse feet, optional

2 metal end caps, optional for drawstring

¾ yard (68.5cm) high-loft fusible fleece, 22"+ (56cm+) wide

¼ yard (23cm) heavyweight interfacing, 20"+ (51cm+) wide

All-purpose thread to match fabrics

Small tube of vinyl adhesive

Hole punch

Permanent marker in a color to match the exterior vinyl

Project Notes

- All your bag hardware should match. Ours were nickel in a bright finish.

- Instead of the metal caps for the drawstring, you can also simply knot the ends. We used belt buckle end caps.

- Measurements are given as width × height.

Getting Started

1. From the exterior fabric, cut the following:

   - 2 rectangles 17" × 19½" (43cm × 49.5cm) for the main panels
   - 1 rectangle 2½" × 1" (6.5cm × 2.5cm) for the drawstring slider
   - 1 strip 1" × 36" (2.5cm × 91.5cm) for the drawstring
   - 1 strip 3" × 54" or WOF (7.5cm × 137cm) for the strap
   - 1 strip 1" × 14" (2.5cm × 35.5cm) for the side tabs

   Note: These last two strips will be subcut to length during construction.

2. From the lining fabric, cut 2 rectangles 17" × 13" (43cm × 33cm).

3. From the fusible fleece, cut 2 rectangles 16¼" × 12⅜" (41.5cm × 31.4cm).

4. From the heavyweight interfacing, cut 1 panel 6" × 10" (15cm × 25.5cm) to stabilize the bag bottom.

Create the Exterior

1. From each bottom corner of each 17" × 19½" (43cm × 49.5cm) main panel rectangle, cut a 3" × 3" (7.5cm × 7.5cm) square (Figure 1).

2. Find the fusible fleece rectangles. Position a fleece panel on the wrong side of each main exterior panel. The fleece should sit 3⅜" (8.6cm) up from the lower raw edge of the fabric and be centered side to side with ⅜" (1cm) of fabric showing along each side.

3. Following the manufacturer's instructions, fuse the fleece in place on each panel.

4. Place the two exterior panels right sides together. Pin along both sides and across the bottom. Use clips instead of pins if working with vinyl.

5. Using a ½" (1.3cm) seam allowance, stitch along both sides and across the bottom; leave the corner cutouts unsewn (Figure 2). We recommend lengthening your stitch when working with vinyl. We used a 3.5mm stitch length.

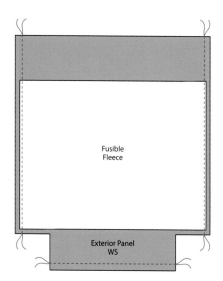

Front Panel
RS

Figure 1

Fusible
Fleece

Exterior Panel
WS

Figure 2

6. Press open the seam allowances as best you can. On vinyl, it can be helpful to work with a pressing ham and pressing cloth for the best results.

7. To create the boxed corner, align each side seam with the bottom seam and pin or clip in place.

8. Using a ½" (1.3cm) seam allowance, stitch across the corner twice for extra reinforcement. Because of the thicker vinyl, we also recommend cutting away the seam allowance and trimming back the seamed edges as close as possible to the stitching (Figure 3).

9. Turn the bag right-side out and push out the corners into position.

10. Fold down the top raw edge of the bag ½" (1.3cm), wrong sides together, and clip in position all the way around.

11. Topstitch this fold in position, running your seam ¼" (6mm) from the top fold (Figure 4).

Note: This seam is essentially a basting seam to hold the vinyl fold in place. However, when the bag is complete with the final line of topstitching, this interior hem will take on the look of a nice, flat-felled seam.

12. Fold down the top, wrong sides together, to create the facing, using the edge of the fleece as your folding guideline. If the vinyl is not laying as flat as you'd like, trim back your side seam allowances to reduce bulk.

13. Clip the fold in place all around.

14. Find the 6" × 10" (15cm × 25.5cm) heavy interfacing panel. Set it down into the base of the bag.

15. If adding the optional purse feet, find them now. Measure ¾" (2cm) in from each corner and use the foot's washer to mark the position for insertion (Figure 5).

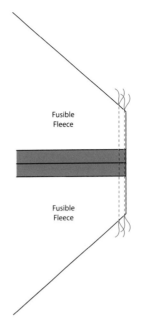

Figure 3

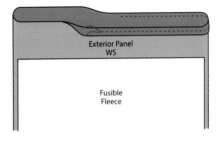

Figure 4

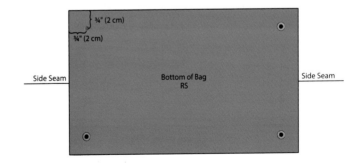

Figure 5

16. Following the manufacturer's instructions, set each foot in place. The feet should insert through the vinyl as well as the heavy interfacing panel at the base of the bag (Figure 6).

17. If you do not use purse feet, we would recommend adhering the heavy interfacing to the bottom of the bag with a fusible seam tape or a fabric adhesive.

18. Set aside the bag exterior.

Create the Lining

1. Find the two lining panels. As above, cut 3" (7.5cm) squares from each bottom corner. Stitch the side seams and bottom seam (Figure 7). Remember to return your machine's stitch length to normal when working with the cotton lining.

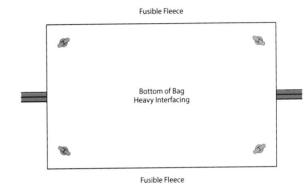

Figure 6

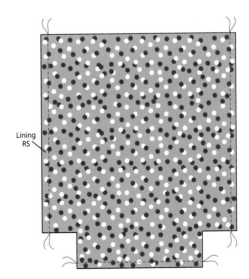

Figure 7

2. Box the corners (Figure 8). Push out the corners, but leave the lining wrong-side out.

3. Find the exterior bag; it should be right-side out. Unfold its top hem.

4. Slip the lining inside the exterior so the two are now wrong sides together. Push the lining all the way down against the base of the exterior, aligning the bottom and side seams. The top raw edge of the lining should sit about 2½" (6.5cm) down from the top edge of the fleece. Pin the lining to the fleece (Figure 9).

5. Fold the top hem back down into position one more time and clip in place.

6. Topstitch the bottom fold of the hem in place all the way around the bag. Your seam should run just about ⅛" (3mm) from the hem's edge (Figure 10). Now you can see the double line of stitching that creates the faux flat-felled seam mentioned above. We stitched along the inside edge of the facing to keep a straight seam. This means your bobbin thread is what shows on the exterior; make sure you thread accordingly.

Attach the Grommets

1. Mark the positions for the twelve grommets that will circle the top of the bag: six along the front and six along the back. To do this, first find the exact center of the bag front by measuring from each side seam.

2. Measure 2¼" (5.5cm) down from the top finished edge of the bag. Measure 1⅛" (2.9cm) to the right of center and 1⅛" (2.9cm) to the left of center. These points create the positions for the first two grommets that will sit to the right and left of center.

3. Working from these first points, place markings for two additional grommets to the right and two additional grommets to the left. These additional grommets should be 2¼" (5.5cm) apart.

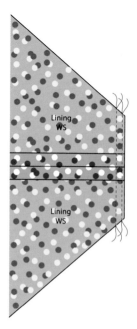

Figure 8

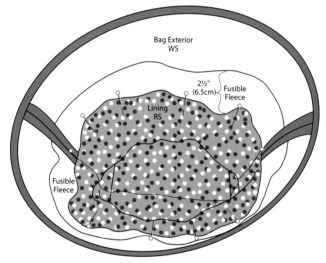

Figure 9

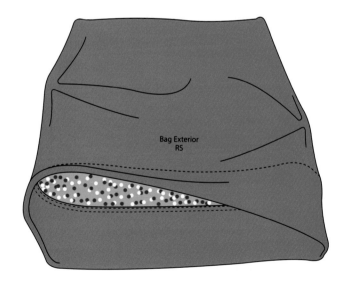

Figure 10

4. Repeat Steps 2–4 to create a matching set of grommet placement marks on the back panel. When complete, there should be 4½" (11.5cm) of space around each side from front grommet to back grommet.

5. Punch a hole at each marked point (Figure 11).

Note: Our measurements for the grommets above, as well as the snaps below, are always given as center point to center point.

6. Set all twelve grommets in place following the manufacturer's instructions.

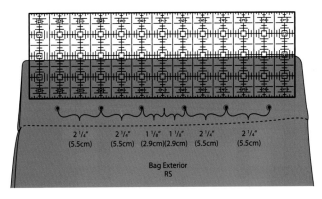

2¼" (5.5cm)   2¼" (5.5cm)   1⅛" (2.9cm)   1⅛" (2.9cm)   2¼" (5.5cm)   2¼" (5.5cm)

Bag Exterior
RS

Figure 11

Create the Straps and Strap Tabs

1. Find the 3" × 54" (7.5cm × 137cm) fabric strip. Subcut the strip into one 31½" (80cm) length and one 22½" (57cm) strip for the bag's longer and shorter shoulder straps.

2. To reduce bulk, clip the corners on both ends at a diagonal.

Note: This clip will leave a small white edge at the very corners, but you can touch it up with the permanent marker.

3. Fold in both sides ½" (1.3cm) and clip in place. Fold up both ends ½" (1.3cm) and clip (Figure 12).

4. Fold each strip in half, wrong sides together, aligning all the pressed edges.

5. Edgestitch around all four sides of both straps (Figure 13).

Note: Be very careful at all the corner pivot points of the straps. If necessary, stop with the needle in the down position and hand walk into and out of the corner pivot.

6. Find the 1" × 14" (2.5cm × 35.5cm) strip. Edgestitch along both 14" (35.5cm) sides, keeping your seam just ⅛" (3mm) from the raw edges of the strip.

7. Trim the ends of the strip to remove any messy start and stop stitching. Then cut the remaining length into two 6" (15cm) tabs.

8. Find the four D-rings. Slip each raw end of each tab through a D-ring, folding the tab back on itself about 1" (2.5cm). Use a dab of the vinyl adhesive to hold the folded-back edges in place; clip to secure until the adhesive dries (Figure 14).

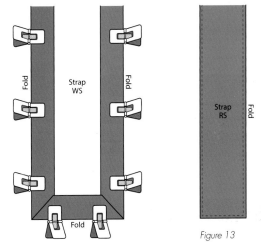

Fold   Strap WS   Fold   Fold

Strap RS   Fold

Fold

Figure 12

Figure 13

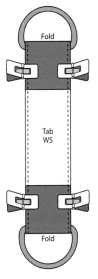

Fold

Tab WS

Fold

Figure 14

9. When dry, place a tab inside the bag at each side seam. The tab should be centered over the seam with the top D-ring extending just above the top fold and the bottom D-ring extending just below the inner-facing fold.

10. Clip the top of the tab to the bag. Gently lift up the tab so you can apply vinyl adhesive to both the bag and the back of the tab. Replace the tab back into position. Re-clip if necessary and allow to fully dry (Figure 15).

11. When dry, secure the bottom end of each tab with a short horizontal seam. This topstitched seam should follow exactly in line with the previous line of stitching that secured the bag's facing. Do not reverse to lock the seam at the beginning or end; simply stitch across. If possible, we recommend using a hump jumper to level the foot.

12. Starting at a seam line, add a final line of topstitching all the way around the top of the bag. This seam secures the top of the tabs and creates a professional finish. It should run about ⅛" (3mm) from the top folded edge (Figure 16). Again, you may want to use a hump jumper to level the presser foot.

13. Touch up the edges of the tabs with the permanent marker.

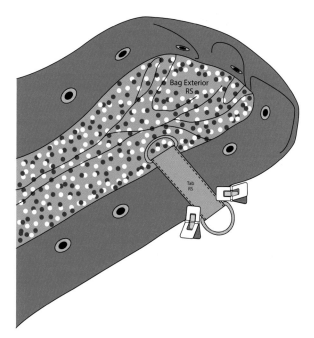

Figure 15

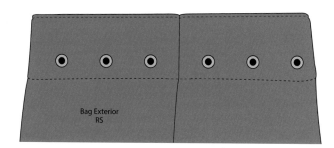

Figure 16

Hump Jumper

A hump jumper is an attachment placed under the back of the presser foot to level the foot for a smooth start to your stitching when you're stitching many layers. Some machines include a hump jumper as a standard accessory, but they can also be purchased separately. You could use a folded up square of fabric as a leveler; however, the solid surface of a hump jumper creates better traction.

Insert the Snaps

1. Mark the straps for the D-ring snaps and three adjustable shoulder snaps. The three shoulder snaps should be centered within the width of each strap, with the first snap 1¼" (3.2cm) in from the finished end and snaps two and three 2¼" (5.5cm) apart.

2. Carefully align both ends so the snaps line up for a perfect fit (Figure 17).

3. At the opposite finished end of each strap, place one additional snap, which will allow the end to loop through the D-ring and snap into place.

4. Center the socket side of each snap within the strap (as you did for the shoulder snaps) and place them 1" (2.5cm) in from the finished end. Center the ball side of each snap within the strap but place them 3¼" (8.5cm) from the finished end (Figure 18).

5. Insert the ends of the strap through the D-rings and snap into place. Then snap together at the shoulder.

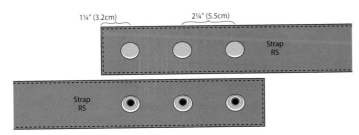

Figure 17

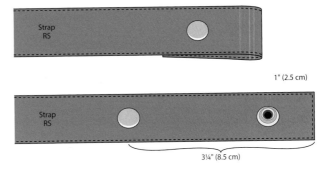

Figure 18

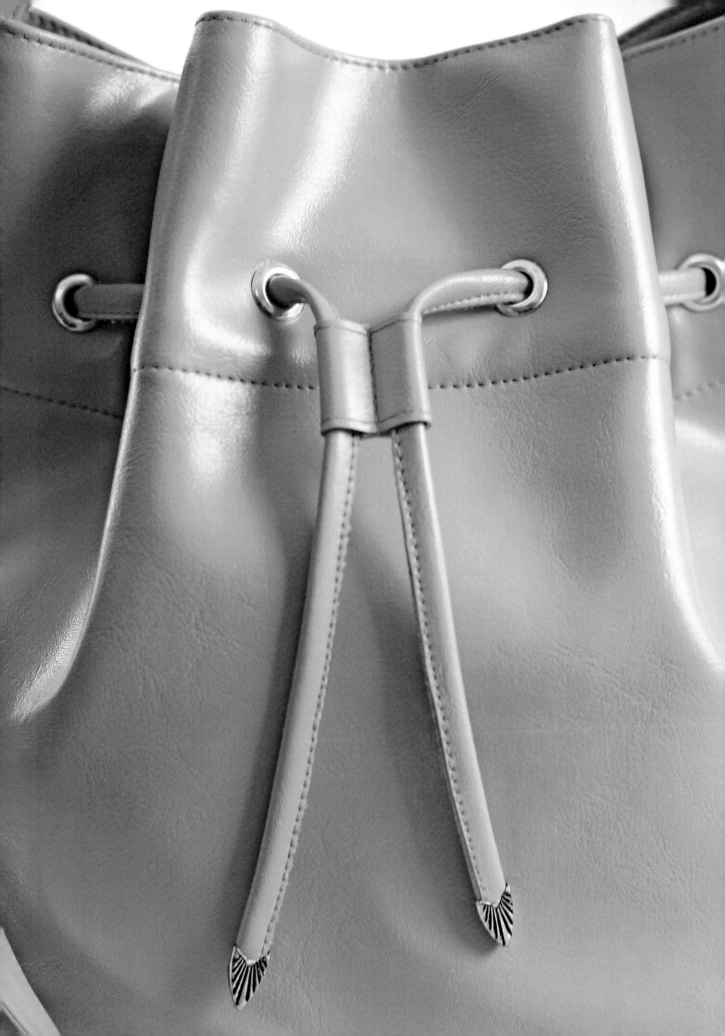

Create the Drawstring and Slider

1. Find the 1" × 36" (2.5cm × 91.5cm) strip. Fold in one 36" (91.5cm) edge ¼" (6mm), then roll over again ¼" (6mm). There will be about ½" (1.3cm) of the strip extending from the roll fold.

2. Edgestitch this narrow hem in place, running your seam as close to the inner fold as possible (Figure 19).

Note: We did not use clips to hold our roll fold. Instead, we simply held the roll as it moved through the machine. However, you could certainly use clips.

3. Using small, sharp scissors, trim away the excess vinyl along the fold (Figure 20).

4. As above with the other raw cut edges, use the permanent marker to touch up the drawstring.

5. Find the 1" × 2½" (2.5cm × 6.5cm) strip. As you did above with the tab strip, edgestitch along both 2½" (6.5cm) sides.

6. Fold in the ends, overlapping them about ¼" (6mm) at the center back to form a small circle. Clip in place.

7. Stitch down the center to secure the overlap and create two openings (Figure 21).

8. As above, touch up the raw sides with the permanent marker.

9. Find the drawstring and the finished bag. You will start with the full 36" (91.5cm) length of drawstring, cutting it to fit.

10. Slip one end of the drawstring through one side of the slider. Then weave this end in and out through the bag's grommets. When you come out through the last grommet, feed the end of the drawstring through the opposite side of the slider (Figure 22).

11. Cinch the bag closed to your desired look. When brand-new, the vinyl will be a bit stiff, so you'll need to work the drawstring through, adjusting as you go to gather up the top. As the bag is used, the vinyl will soften and will open and close more easily. When the bag is closed to your satisfaction, trim away about 5" (12.5cm) from each end of the drawstring. You may trim slightly more or slightly less; the finished look is up to you.

12. If using end caps, trim each end into a point. Place a dot of glue on the tip and slide the cord into the end caps. Gently crimp in place with needle-nose pliers. You can also simply cut each end on the diagonal and knot to finish.

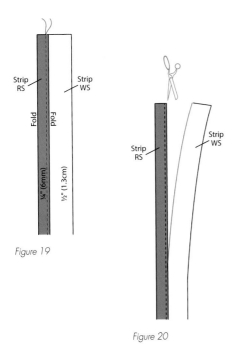

Figure 19

Figure 20

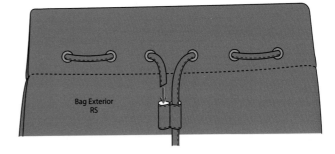

Figure 21

Figure 22

Resources

Below are a few favorite manufacturers we turn to for the fabric, notions and hardware to complete our bag projects. Bear in mind that fabric collections, like fashion, change each season. The exact fabric used for the samples shown in this book may no longer be readily available. We've listed the major manufacturer websites, although most do not sell to the public. They do, however, often provide a dealer locator list, or you can simply look for these top brand names at your favorite local shop or online retailer. In addition to the companies listed below, we also turn to etsy.com quite often to find unique hardware, buttons, purse frames, specialty zippers and more.

Fabric

Art Gallery Fabrics
www.artgalleryfabrics.com

Cotton + Steel
www.cottonandsteelfabrics.com

FreeSpirit Fabrics
freespiritfabric.com

Michael Miller Fabrics
www.michaelmillerfabrics.com

Moda Fabrics
storefront.unitednotions.com

Premier Prints
www.premierprintsinc.com

Shannon Fabrics
www.shannonfabrics.com

Notions and Hardware

Buckle Guy
www.buckleguy.com

Prym Consumer USA (Dritz)
www.dritz.com

Purse Supply Depot
www.pursesupplydepot.com

Zipit
www.etsy.com/shop/zipit

Tools

Oliso Irons
www.oliso.com/smartiron

Janome Sewing Machines
janome.com

Sew4Home

To support your technique development, we've created full tutorials to show you step by step how to work our techniques. For more information, visit sew4home.com and search any one of the topics listed below.

Hand Stitching Basics

How to Fussy Cut Fabric Motifs

How to Box Corners

How to Insert a Magnetic Snap Closure

How to Install Metal Grommets

How to Insert a Turn or Twist Lock Closure

How to Install a Conventional Zipper

How to Make Knife Pleats

How to Sew a Perfect X Box

Sewing Smooth Curves Every Time

Stitching and Cutting Corners Correctly

Index

a content + ecommerce company

20   19   18   17   16   5   4   3   2   1

Distributed in Canada by Fraser Direct
100 Armstrong Avenue
Georgetown, ON, Canada L7G 5S4
Tel: (905) 877-4411

Distributed in the U.K. and Europe by F&W MEDIA INTERNATIONAL
Brunel House, Newton Abbot, Devon, TQ12 4PU, England
Tel: (+44) 1626 323200, Fax: (+44) 1626 323319
E-mail: enquiries@fwmedia.com

SRN: T8812
ISBN-13: 978-1-4402-4504-6

PDF SRN: T8821
PDF ISBN-13: 978-1-4402-4513-8

Edited by Christine Doyle
Designed by Nicola DosSantos
Photography by Deana Travers
Illustrations by Sue Friend

© Istockphoto.com/novaaleksandra
Stock vector ID:83535213

Metric Conversion Chart		
To Convert	To	Multiply By
Inches	Centimeters	2.54
Centimeters	Inches	0.4
Feet	Centimeters	30.5
Centimeters	Feet	0.03
Yards	Meters	0.9
Meters	Yards	1.1

About the Authors

Creative Director Anne Adams and Senior Editor Liz McKinney-Johnson head up the *Sew4Home* team of industry professionals from headquarters in Portland, Oregon, the creative hub of the Pacific Northwest. The sisters started Sew4Home.com in 2009 as a site for creatively active do-it-yourselfers who were looking to make unique, stylish items for their homes and families.

Both Anne and Liz come from backgrounds in the world of marketing and design, so first and foremost, they knew Sew4Home.com had to be a site people would turn to for the latest trends, the hottest fabrics and the best tools to put them all together. Second, they wanted to be able to send their visitors to find the exact products they used in their tutorials. Third, they knew every article had to be thoroughly written, beautifully presented and fun! If they were having fun, visitors would be having fun too … and experiencing the thrill of creating something wonderful with their own two hands.

Today, thousands of visitors from around the world stop by *Sew4Home* every day to see what's new. But even with all the growth and success, Anne and Liz never stop delighting in comments like this from new sewers: "My project turned out awesome. Thank you so much. I can't wait to make more. I am so proud of myself!"

Dedication

This book is dedicated to all the loyal followers who have supported us over the years and brought the site to where it is today. There are so many choices out there in the creative realm, and we so appreciate that you keep us on the top of your go-to list. We also dedicate this book to our mom, Sally. She taught us hard work won't kill you, there's beauty in what's simple and true, and if you don't stop scratching, it will never heal. Love you, Mom.

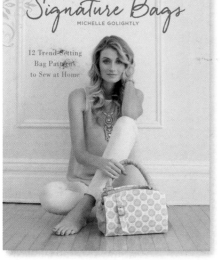
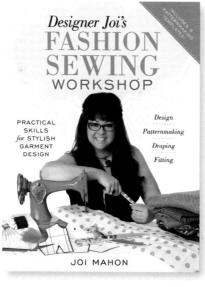
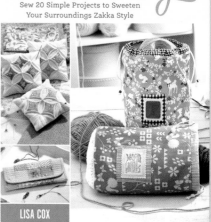